NASA scientists have studied the tufa towers at **Mono Lake** in California, U.S.A., for decades, as similar rock formations are also **found on Mars.**

NATIONAL
GEOGRAPHIC
KiDS

That's Fact-tastic!

Mind-Blowing, Eye-Popping, Jaw-Dropping Stuff About Our World

NATIONAL GEOGRAPHIC
WASHINGTON, D.C.

Contents

Amazing Amazon Rainforest

Facts

1

The **harpy eagle,** which preys on monkeys and sloths, has **talons** larger than a **grizzly bear's** claws.

2

The **toco toucan** can adjust blood flow into its **large bill,** allowing the bird to **keep cool** in the tropical heat.

3

Capybara, the world's **largest rodents,** look like their guinea pig relatives but are the size of a Saint Bernard.

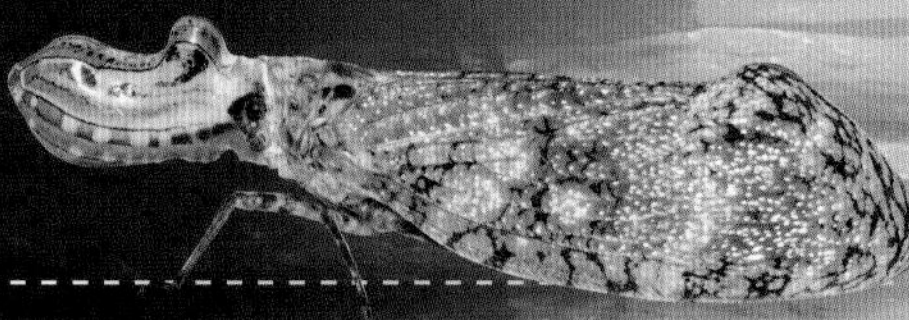

4

The **peanut-head bug,** which lives on the Amazon **forest floor,** has a **head** that looks like an unshelled **peanut.**

5

A **glass frog's** belly is see-through, so you can see its heart beating.

6

The Amazon rainforest is **twice the size** of India.

7

Some parts of the Amazon get **400 inches** (1,016 cm) of **rainfall** a year.

8

After seasonal rains, the **Amazon River** floods forests, allowing freshwater Amazon river dolphins to swim **among the trees.**

9

The green anaconda, the **world's heaviest snake,** weighs more than a **mountain gorilla.**

10

The Amazon is so **dense with vegetation** that it can take **rain** 10 minutes for to reach the ground.

Strong Facts

About the Human

skeleton

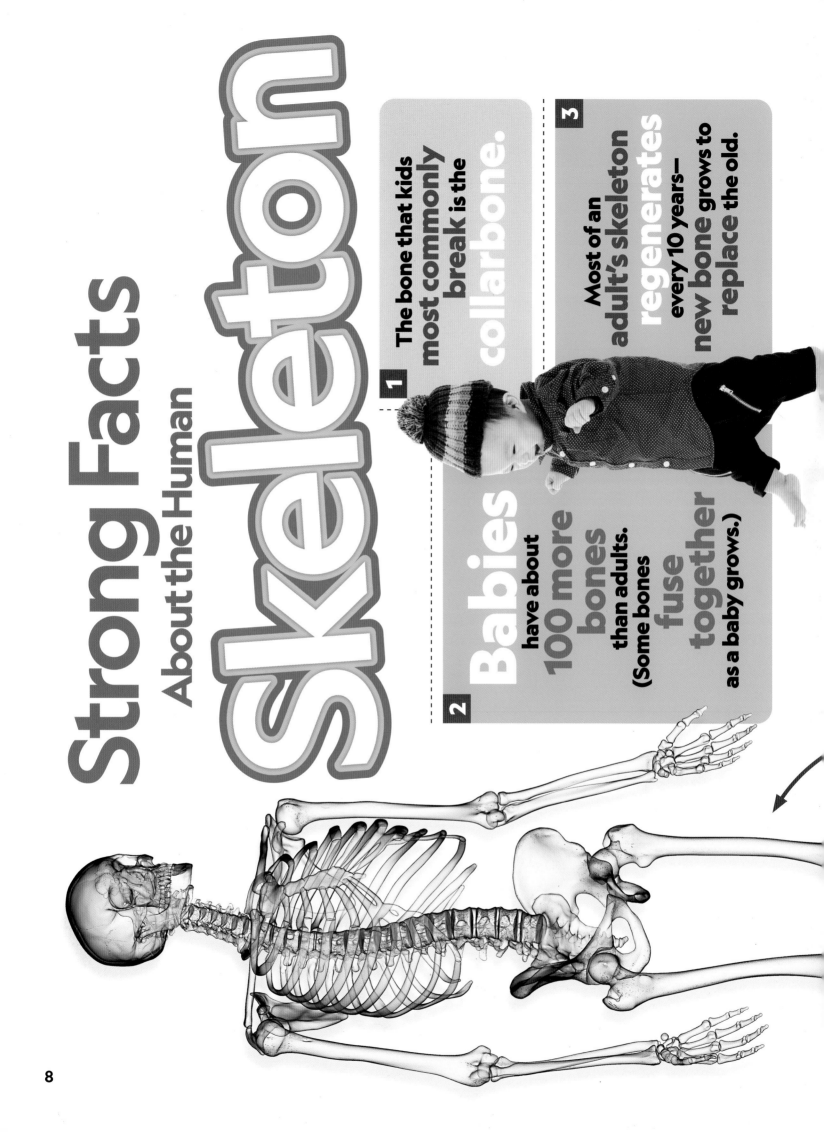

1

The bone that kids most commonly break is the **collarbone.**

2

Babies

have about **100 more bones** than adults. (Some bones **fuse together** as a baby grows.)

3

Most of an adult's skeleton **regenerates** every 10 years— new bone grows to replace the old.

4

The **thighbone** is the longest and strongest bone in the body.

5

The **funny bone** isn't actually a bone— it's a nerve that runs inside your elbow.

6

The average **adult skeleton** weighs **20 pounds** (9 kg).

7

The bones in your **hands and wrists** make up about a quarter of all the bones in your body.

8

The **smallest bone** in your body, located in your middle ear, is about half as long as a grain of rice.

9

The hyoid is the only bone in your body **not connected** to another one— it's located at the base of your tongue.

10

Teeth are part of the **skeletal system,** and the enamel that covers them is **stronger than bone.**

Spacecraft

Facts That

Blast Off

1

Astronauts on the International **Space Station** season their food with **liquid salt** and **pepper—** grains might **float away** and clog the air vents.

The legs of Robonaut 2, a **humanoid robot** designed to work **alongside astronauts** on the International Space Station, are **nine feet** (2.7 m) long when fully extended.

2

3
In 1990, Voyager 1 took the **first and only photograph** of our **solar system.**

4
Sleeping bags on the International Space Station are **tied to the walls** so that the astronauts won't float around the room while they sleep.

5
In 2018, the spacecraft company SpaceX **launched** a **red convertible car** into space.

6
During its **nine years in space,** the Kepler Space Telescope **discovered** more than **2,600 planets** outside our solar system.

7
The **space shuttle** can go from zero to **17,000 miles an hour** (27,360 km/h) in 8.5 minutes—that's **100 times faster** than the **fastest race cars.**

8
On its final flybys of the sun in 2025, the **Parker Solar Probe,** a spacecraft sent to gather data about the **sun's surface,** will travel 430,000 miles an hour (692,000 km/h)—fast enough to get from Tokyo, Japan, to New York, U.S.A., in **less than a minute.**

9
Mars rovers practice for their missions in Chile's **Atacama Desert** because that's the place on Earth most similar to **Mars.**

10
The Mars rover Perseverance is looking for **signs that life—** in the form of microbes— **once existed** on the **red planet.**

11

What's the Difference?

Check out these similar pairings and see how you can determine this from that!

INSECT VS. ARACHNID VS. BUG

Not all "bugs" are *really* bugs. Scientists categorize these creatures into three different groups: insects, arachnids, and true bugs. Here's how to sort them out. Insect bodies have three parts: a head, a middle section (called a thorax), and an abdomen. They have a hard external skeleton, or exoskeleton, and antennae, and adults have six legs. At some point in their life, most insects have wings. Bees, beetles, flies, and wasps are all insects. Arachnids are quite different from insects. Arachnid bodies have only two sections, an abdomen and a combined head and thorax. They have neither antennae nor wings, and they have eight legs. Spiders, scorpions, and ticks are arachnids. A "true bug" is a type of insect, but not all insects are true bugs. The main thing that separates a true bug from other insects is its mouth. True bugs include aphids, bedbugs, and stink bugs.

Stinkbug

LEGEND VS. MYTH

Once upon a time ... Two of the oldest types of stories are legends and myths. Legends are usually based on a real person or event. However, the story often changes and the facts become exaggerated. Tales of brave people and extraordinary deeds are told and retold for many years. Soon, the story—the legend—is bigger than the person or event that inspired it. Stories about King Arthur and Robin Hood are legends based on real people (who may not have been much like their legendary characters at all). Myths, on the other hand, aren't based on real people or events. They are often stories made up to explain things people didn't understand well, such as how the world came to be or why birds can fly. Unlike legends, which are about humans, myths are usually about gods or other supernatural creatures. The stories of Greek gods, goddesses, and heroes are examples of myths.

BISON VS. BUFFALO

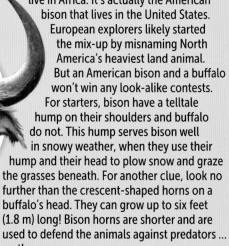
Water buffalo

The confusion begins with the lyrics of the classic folk song about the American West, "Home on the Range": "Oh, give me a home, where the buffalo roam / Where the deer and the antelope play ..." Here's the problem: There aren't any buffalo in the United States. Water buffalo live in South Asia, and African buffalo live in Africa. It's actually the American bison that lives in the United States. European explorers likely started the mix-up by misnaming North America's heaviest land animal. But an American bison and a buffalo won't win any look-alike contests. For starters, bison have a telltale hump on their shoulders and buffalo do not. This hump serves bison well in snowy weather, when they use their hump and their head to plow snow and graze the grasses beneath. For another clue, look no further than the crescent-shaped horns on a buffalo's head. They can grow up to six feet (1.8 m) long! Bison horns are shorter and are used to defend the animals against predators ... on the range.

HIKING VS. TREKKING

Hiking and trekking are both great ways to get outside and explore the world on foot. So why are there two names for taking a walk? The terms overlap a little, but don't let the differences trip you up. Hiking usually means walking in the woods or on trails. A hike might last for several hours, and you can take one on a moment's notice—just lace up your boots, fill up your water bottle, and head for the trails. Trekking, on the other hand, involves a few more steps. A trek often lasts several days. It requires more planning and more gear. But many people use the word "hike" for both types of walking adventures. A hike can be as long and as challenging as a trek. The word "trek," however, isn't often used for a short stroll in the woods.

SORBET VS. SHERBET

A big scoop of cold, fruity sorbet or sherbet makes a refreshing, sweet treat on a hot summer day. You may not care which your bowl holds, as long as it melts in your mouth, but these two frozen desserts are different. Sorbet is made with only fruit and sugar. This keeps the treat yummy but light. Sherbet is a little richer and creamier. It has fruit and sugar, too, but also a small amount of milk or cream and maybe some eggs or gelatin. Now when you visit the snack stand at the beach, you'll know just what's in your favorite scoop.

Sorbet

STAR VS. PLANET

When you look up at the night sky, you see a sprinkling of glowing lights. Many of these are stars, but some are planets. What's the difference? A star is a giant ball of flaming gases, mostly hydrogen and helium. Inside a star, hydrogen atoms and helium atoms collide, or bump into each other. These collisions create a huge amount of energy. This energy is what makes a star glow. More than 100 billion stars twinkle in our galaxy, the Milky Way. Stars make their own light, but planets don't—they can only reflect light from stars. Planets move in a fixed orbit around a star, and in our solar system, that star is the sun. So when you see a planet in the night sky, it appears to glow because it is reflecting light from the sun. But how can you tell a star from a planet when you're looking at the sky from Earth? Stars twinkle. Planets don't.

Wondrous
Facts About
Natural Wonders

1

The **northern lights** make sounds—described as crackles or **muffled bangs**—that can be heard from the ground.

2

You can **hear** the rushing water of **Victoria Falls** from a mile (1.6 km) away.

Dead Sea

3

The **Eye of the Sahara,** a geological formation that can be seen from space, is sometimes **used as a** **landmark** by **astronauts.**

4

The **Dead Sea** is not totally dead— fish and plants can't survive, but **bacteria,** **algae, and fungi** thrive.

5 The **giant sequoias** in California, U.S.A., are **resistant** to disease and can live up to **3,000 years.**

6 The **Great Barrier Reef** covers about the same area as **70 million soccer fields.**

7 **Split Apple Rock,** or Tokangawhā, is a **120-million-year-old** granite **boulder** off the coast of New Zealand that may have been used as an ancient astronomical **calendar.**

8 **Wind speeds** at the summit of **Mount Everest** can be **stronger** than those in a category 5 **hurricane.**

9 The Galápagos Islands have been called a **"living museum"** because of the **unique animals** found there, such as the **giant tortoise.**

10 There's **one town** inside the **Grand Canyon** in Arizona, U.S.A.—it can only be reached by **hiking, riding an animal,** or flying in **by helicopter.**

3

Dogs don't always say **"woof"**: In Iceland they say **"voff,"** and in Romania it's **"ham."**

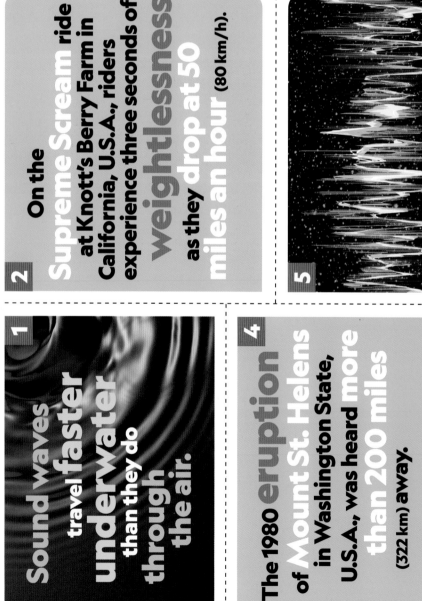

6

To make sure cars **could hear him** as he biked, a man in London, England, invented the Hornster, a horn louder than a jet engine.

2

On the **Supreme Scream** ride at Knott's Berry Farm in California, U.S.A., riders experience three seconds of **weightlessness** as they drop at 50 miles an hour (80 km/h).

5

A **black hole** in the Perseus Cluster, some 250 million light-years away, **"hums"** a sound about one million billion times lower than any human can hear.

1

Sound waves **travel faster underwater** than they do through the air.

4

The 1980 **eruption** of Mount St. Helens in Washington State, U.S.A., was heard more than 200 miles (322 km) away.

7

Cicadas create their **loud buzzing** by "buckling" two tymbals, organs on their exoskeletons, like an accordion.

Earsplitting
Facts About
Sound

8

A pet cat named Merlin once purred about as loud as a **vacuum cleaner.**

9

Male white **bellbirds,** which live in the Amazon rainforest, can sing **as loud** as an **ambulance siren.**

10

Elephants make **low rumbles** in their throats that travel for about 3.5 miles (5.6 km) underground and are so strong that humans can **feel the vibrations.**

17

A baby dugong—a relative of manatees—may **catch a ride** on its **mother's back.**

1

2 **Harp seals** get their name from the **harp-shaped ring** on the **adults' backs.**

3 Beluga whales **rub up against rocks** to shed their skin.

4 When harbor porpoises **come up for air,** they make a **puffing noise** that **sounds like a sneeze.**

5 **Walruses** have **air sacs** in their necks that act like **life preservers** to help them float.

6 **A newborn otter's** extra-thick fur makes it **impossible** for the little one **to sink.**

7 The lungs of the sperm whale are **designed to collapse** to withstand the **pressure** of its **deep dives.**

Facts About Marine Mammals to Dive Into

9 A **newborn blue whale** weighs more than an **adult hippopotamus.**

10 **Polar bears,** which live most of their life on sea ice, have a **thick layer of body fat**—up to **four inches (10 cm)**— that keeps them warm.

8 Scientists can tell what a leopard seal **has eaten** by analyzing the chemicals in its **whiskers.**

Basketball

Facts You Can Take to the Hoop

1 The **U.S. Supreme Court** building has a **basketball court** on the top floor.

2 The NBA's Philadelphia **76ers** got their name because the Declaration of Independence was signed in the city in **1776.**

3 Golden State Warrior **Stephen Curry** has been **fined $100 by his mom** for **each turnover** he makes after his third in a game.

4 Former NBA star **Shaquille O'Neal** wears **size 22 shoes.**

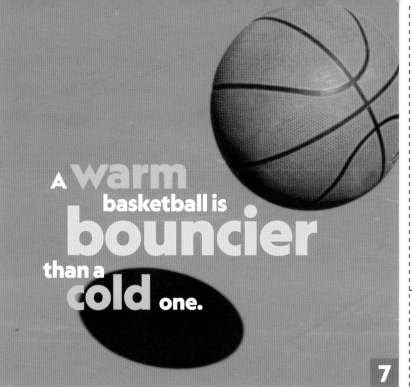

A **warm** basketball is **bouncier** than a **cold** one.

7

Basketball was **first played** using **soccer balls.**

5

The **longest** successful **basketball shot** measured **112 feet 6 inches (34.3 m),** longer than the **entire length** of a court.

8

6

The first basketball **hoops** were **peach baskets.**

9

Regardless of experience, American men have a **17 percent chance** of **playing for the NBA** if they are **7 feet** (2 m) or taller.

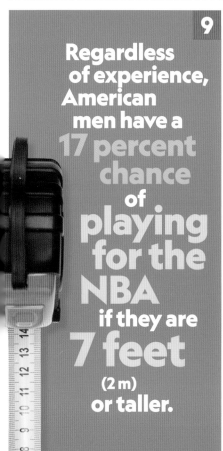

10

Dribbling was **not originally** part of the game—players could only **move the ball** by **passing it.**

Awesome
Facts About
Amphibians

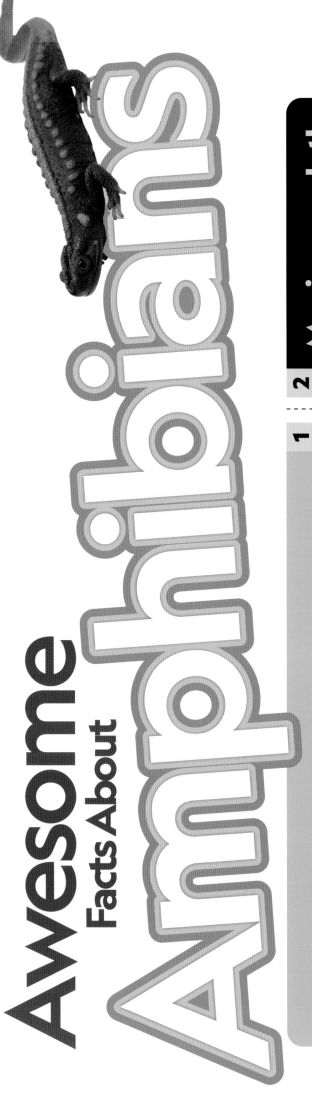

2 Mexican axolotls (ACK-suh-LAH-tuhls), a kind of salamander, can **regrow lost body parts.**

1 The more than 8,000 species of amphibians on Earth are **cold-blooded** animals that breathe through their thin skin.

5

Tadpoles have **tiny teeth** they use to eat pond plants.

6

The word **"amphibian"** comes from the Greek words for **"both kinds of life,"** since most live part of their life in **water and part on land.**

10

Amphibian teeth are used to **hold prey but not to chew it**—amphibians swallow their food **whole.**

4

The world's largest caecilian lives in Colombia and grows to be nearly **five feet long**—that's taller than the average 11-year-old. (1.5 m)

3

Skin almost completely **covers the eyes** of some underground caecilian (sih-SIL-yen) species.

8

About the size of a bowling ball, the **armored devil toad** lived alongside the dinosaurs and weighed a whopping 10 pounds (4.5 kg).

7

Poison frogs belong to the family Dendrobatidae, which means **"tree-walker"** in Latin.

9

Some people think the squeaky sound made by salamanders known as **mudpuppies** is similar to a **dog's bark.**

Turn the page for more amazing amphibian facts!

13

The Siberian newt can **hibernate in frozen ground** because it produces special chemicals that protect it from extreme cold.

15

Caecilians are the only amphibians with **tentacles.**

12

A study found that olms, aquatic salamanders that live in **flooded caves** in Bosnia and Herzegovina, move just a few feet over several years.

11

African clawed frogs can **stay in the mud** at the bottom of dried-out ponds for a year while waiting for the rains to return.

14

A giant cane toad found in Australia was nicknamed **"Toadzilla"** because it was about the size of a **small dog.**

17

Great crested newts, which live only in Europe, produce a **foul-smelling,** milky substance to keep predators away.

16

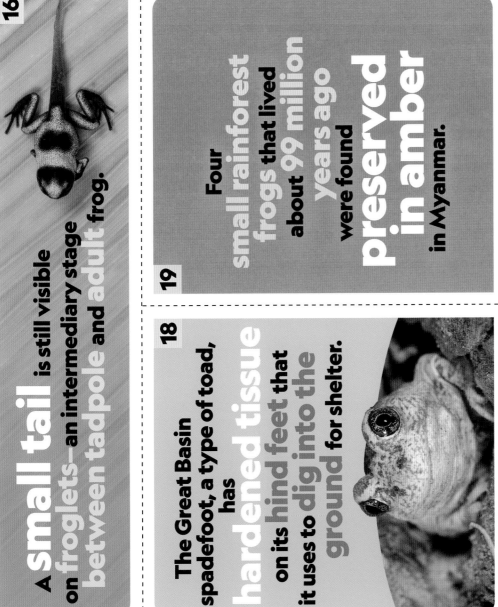

A **small tail** is still visible on froglets—an intermediary stage between tadpole and adult frog.

19

Four **small rainforest frogs** that lived **about 99 million years ago** were found **preserved in amber** in Myanmar.

18

The Great Basin spadefoot, a type of toad, has **hardened tissue** on its hind feet that it uses to **dig into the ground** for shelter.

20

Poisonous mantella frogs— small, brightly colored frogs found only on the island of Madagascar—get their toxins from the flies, ants, and termites they eat.

Super Sharp
Facts About
Cheese

1

In Albertville, France, the town's **electricity** is **generated** by using whey—a by-product of **cheesemaking**—to produce methane gas.

2

It takes about **five quarts** (4.7 L) of **cow's or goat's milk** to make one **pound** (0.5 kg) of **cheese.**

3

Cheese **may help prevent cavities.**

4

Some **cheeses** are treated with **edible mold** to help them **develop flavor.**

5

In 1835, a dairy farmer gave President Andrew Jackson a **1,400-pound** (635-kg) **cheese** that was said to have remained in the White House for **two years.**

6

A law in Wisconsin, U.S.A., once **required** restaurants to **serve cheese** with **meals.**

7

The cartoon characters **Wallace and Gromit** created a **boom** in international sales of the British cheese **Wensleydale** because Wallace liked it so much.

You can **make cheese from nuts.**

8

9

Scientists have **made cheese using bacteria** taken from human **toes** and **belly buttons.**

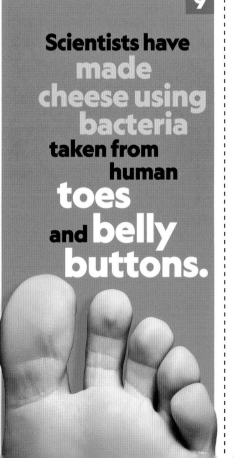

10

The **holes** in Swiss cheese are **called eyes.**

27

Certain cabbage-like plants feel the vibrations of an animal chewing on their leaves and release a chemical to fend off the creature.

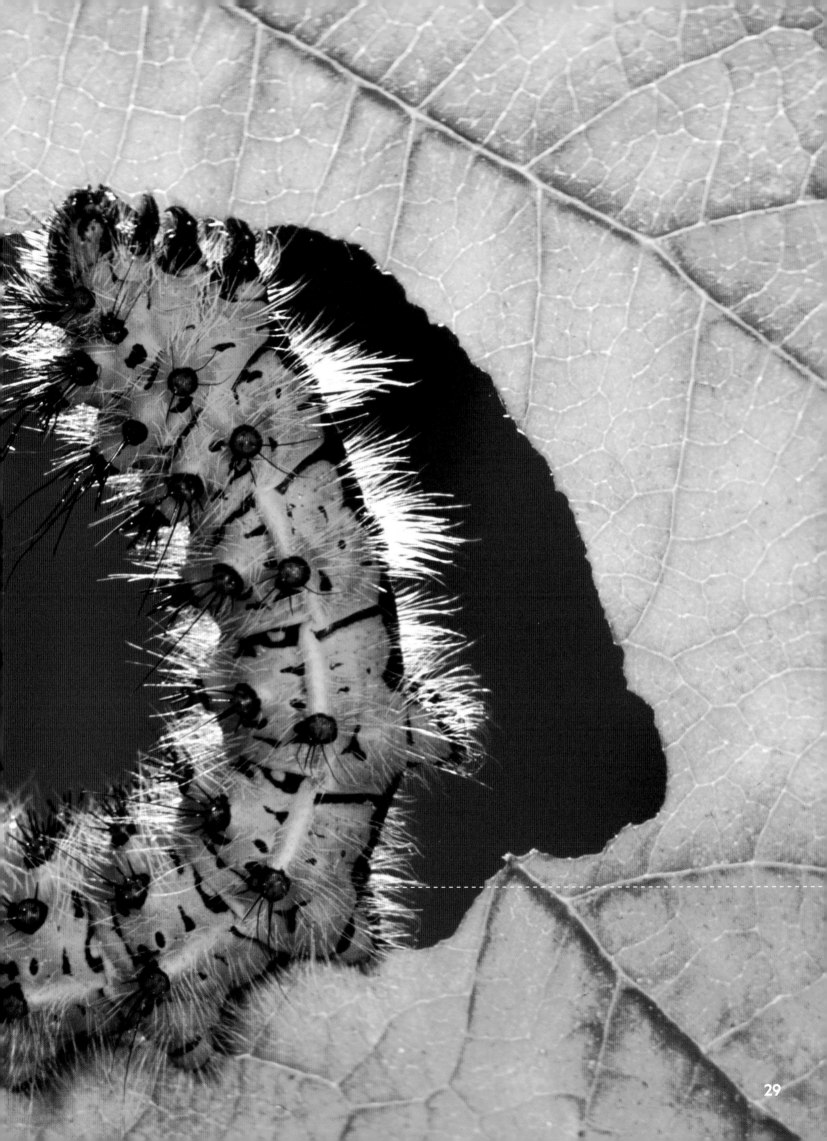

Spicy
Facts to Make Your Eyes Water

1

Kimchi, a spicy Korean dish, was originally made by letting **vegetables age** over the winter in earthen pots buried **in the ground.**

2

The **extremely hot pepper named Pepper X** is more than **1,200 times hotter** than a jalapeño.

3

The ancient Aztec ruler **Montezuma** reportedly drank more than 50 cups a day of *xocoatl,* a **chocolate drink** sometimes flavored with **chili peppers.**

4 Products made from **capsaicin**—which gives **chili peppers** their spice—are used to **keep deer, voles,** and **birds away** from gardens and crops.

5 A **chili pepper's heat** is given in units that measure how much sugar water to add to a **pepper's oil** until you **can't taste its heat.**

6  **Sriracha** hot sauce is named for the coastal city of **Si Racha, Thailand,** where the sauce was **first made.**

7 Scientists created the **Dragon's Breath** pepper not to eat but to add to a **pain-relieving** skin cream.

8 You can **taste garlic** with **your feet.**

9 Hot sauce was first **advertised for sale** in the United States in 1807, and today more than **$1.5 billion** of the spicy condiment is sold **every year.**

10 Since people have different numbers of **taste buds,** spicy foods can taste **hotter to one person** than to another.

1 In a study of 500 people, a researcher found that the more time spent outdoors on a sunny day in spring, the happier the subjects said they felt.

2 People visit the Temple of the Sun and the Temple of the Moon outside Mexico City, Mexico, to celebrate the spring equinox, when the sun aligns with the Equator.

3 In the fall, a special layer of cells forms on tree leaf stems, cutting off nutrients to the leaves and causing them to eventually fall.

4 The phrase "dog days of summer" comes from the ancient Greeks and Romans, who thought that Sirius (known as the dog star), which rises before the sun in late July, added a little extra heat to the sun.

5 If Earth wasn't tilted on its axis, there would be minor temperature changes throughout the year but no seasons.

Sensational Facts About Seasons

6 In Tromsø, Norway, located about 200 miles (322 km) north of the Arctic Circle, the **sun doesn't rise** from November to January.

7 The ancient Egyptians **divided the year** into **three seasons** based on the Nile: when the **river flooded,** when farmers **planted crops,** and when the crops were **harvested.**

8 In early Anglo-Saxon cultures, **age was counted by how many winters** you lived through.

9 During the annual **monsoon season in the tropics, some mice "hitch" rides** on the back of frogs so that they don't get caught in floods.

10 **Seasons on Uranus** last for about **21 Earth years.**

Fun Facts

About

Toys & Games

1

Ancient Greeks used what we now call **Hula-Hoops** as a form of **exercise.**

2

In 1993, Tetris became **the first video game in space** when Russian cosmonaut Aleksandr Serebrov played it on the Mir space station.

3

The United States National Security Agency once **banned Furbies** from its offices because it was thought the talking toys might leak classified information.

4

Play-Doh was invented in the 1930s to help clean soot left by coal-burning furnaces off household walls.

Turn the page for more fun facts!

7

Barbie's

full name is Barbara Millicent Roberts.

6

The Little Tikes **Cozy Coupe** toy car has often outsold some of the most popular real cars.

8

McDonald's is the world's largest **toy distributor.**

10

The biggest **Hot Wheels** track loop ever built was 12 feet 8 inches (3.86 m) tall.

5

During **World War II,** the British government sent money, compasses, files, and maps hidden in **Monopoly games** to help their soldiers escape from German prisoner of war camps.

9

The original **Mr. Potato Head,** created in the United States in 1952, came with eyes, arms, legs, and a mustache—but you had to provide the potato.

11 A Rubik's Cube has **43 quintillion** possible combinations.

12 In Denmark, a contest offered a **lucky winner** the chance to spend the night in a house made **entirely of Legos.**

13 U.S. soldiers **used Slinkys** as **radio antennas** during the Vietnam War.

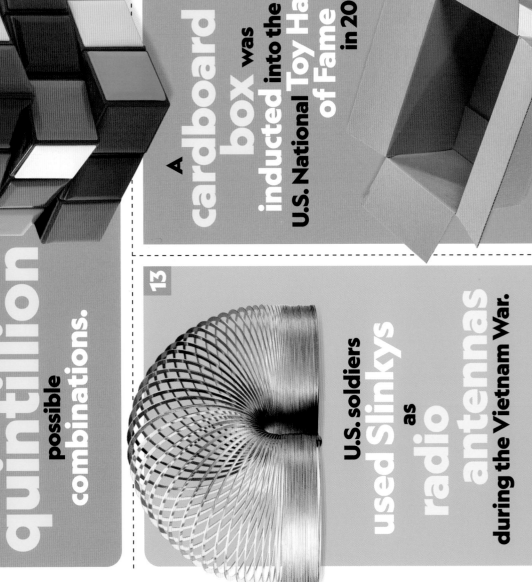

14 A **cardboard box** was **inducted into the** U.S. National Toy Hall of Fame in 2005.

15 A company sold an **edible version** of Candy Land— the playing cards were **made of chocolate.**

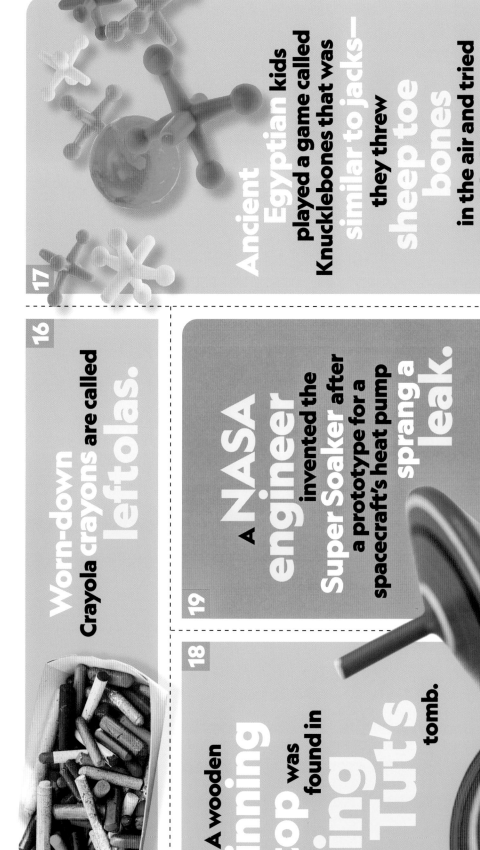

17 Ancient Egyptian kids played a game called Knucklebones that was similar to jacks— they threw **sheep toe bones** in the air and tried to catch them.

20 Astronauts onboard Apollo 8 used **Silly Putty** to hold down tools in **zero gravity.**

16 Worn-down Crayola crayons are called **leftolas.**

19 A NASA engineer invented the Super Soaker after a prototype for a spacecraft's heat pump sprang a **leak.**

18 A wooden **spinning top** was found in **King Tut's** tomb.

Shipshape Facts
About Life
On Board

1

For centuries, **sailors ate biscuits** called **hardtack** that could **last for years—** but sometimes they had to **pick out maggots** first.

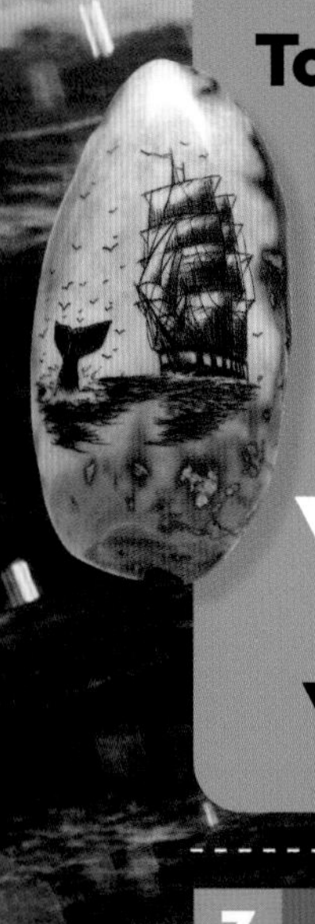

2

To **pass the time** on 18th-century whaling ships, seamen created scrimshaw— **designs engraved** into **whale teeth** and rubbed with **black ink.**

3

Nearly as long as a **blue whale,** a **Viking longship** carried some **32 oarsmen** to row the boat **during expeditions** or to bring soldiers to battle.

4 Early sailors sang rhythmic **sea shanties** to help **ease the dullness** of **repetitive tasks** on board.

5 When there are **more people than bunks** on a ship, sailors take turns sleeping in the **same bed,** a practice known as hot bunking or **hot racking.**

7 Sailors used to plug **leaks** with sections of **old rope mixed with tar.**

8 In the late 1600s, sailors went to the bathroom on **"seats of ease"** located on either side of a ship's bow—their waste **dropped through pipes** down into the water.

9 Naturalist **Charles Darwin's** H.M.S. *Beagle* was so **crowded** that he slept in a hammock strung above a drafting table.

6 **Nuclear submarines** are **so cramped** that spaces often serve **two purposes:** The officers' dining room is a makeshift **hospital,** and the torpedo room is the **workout room.**

10 In 1753, Scottish naval surgeon James Lind showed that **drinking lemon** and **orange juice** could **prevent scurvy,** a disease caused by a vitamin deficiency and often suffered by sailors on long voyages.

Weird water, freaky flies, and mysterious towers rise up in Mono Lake.

Strange gray towers rise from a desert lake reaching skyward like clusters of stout trees. These odd structures may look like living things, but they're not—they're rock formations that "grew" in Mono Lake in California, U.S.A. And they're not the only strange things in the weird water of this curious lake.

ODD AQUATIC LIFE

The lake's salt and natural chemicals make its water inhospitable for fish and other common aquatic creatures, but it's still packed with bizarre life. Trillions of tiny brine shrimp about the size of your fingernail make the lake look like a giant bowl of shrimp soup. Just as abundant—and even weirder—are Mono Lake's freaky alkali flies. They can surround themselves with an air pocket that allows them to "scuba dive" underwater to feed on algae and lay their eggs. The eggs hatch as larvae, which feed underwater. Eventually each larva encases itself in a pupa to change into an adult fly. When it's ready to emerge from its hard pupa, its head splits apart, and a balloonlike structure inside inflates to blow open the pupa. Then its head reassembles, and the adult fly floats to the surface. Mono Lake has more life living in it than most freshwater lakes, and hungry birds know it. Some nest near the all-you-can-eat buffet of shrimp and flies, while migrating birds like phalaropes make pit stops to refuel before their 3,000-mile (4,828-km)-long migration to South America.

WET AND WEIRD

Birds love the brine shrimp, but they won't find any fish in Mono Lake. The lake's nearly three times saltier than the ocean and has an extremely high pH level—a measure of how acidic or alkaline something is. Lifeguards keep the pH level in pools at about seven on the pH scale—to help keep swimmers' eyes comfortable. Mono Lake, which is very alkaline (the opposite of acidic), measures about 10, which is high. "In terms of its pH level, it's a lot like glass cleaner," says Bartshé Miller, education director of the Mono Lake Committee. It might be deadly for fish, but for human swimmers Mono Lake is safe—and weird. The lake water is so loaded with minerals that people float like corks. "It's pretty amazing," Miller says. "You could read a book floating on your back." Swimmer, beware though: The water has a bitter taste and feels greasy.

TOWERING BELOW

The rocky towers that today appear above water originally formed underwater. Freshwater springs gurgling up from the bottom carry calcium, which reacts with the carbonate in the lake water and creates tufa, a kind of rock that contains a lot of calcium carbonate. As the springs flow, the resulting tufa gradually grows. Decades later the tufa becomes a tower as tall as 30 feet (9 m). Groups of tufa towers are visible above the surface because Mono Lake's water level has gone down since they formed.

SAVING A LAKE

Mono Lake may seem like an eco-wasteland, but it's actually an environmental success story. In the 1940s the city of Los Angeles began using some of the water that supplies Mono Lake, and the water level dropped dangerously low. "If the diversion of water continued, Mono Lake would have become a kind of chemical puddle with no life in it," Miller says. But in the 1990s, Los Angeles agreed to use less water to keep Mono Lake alive. "This is a place where the idea of protecting the environment was balanced with the needs of a city," Miller says. "That doesn't always happen, but we achieved it here."

HOW MONO LAKE FORMED

Streams feed Mono Lake, but no water flows out. Over hundreds of thousands of years, evaporation caused minerals carried in by that water to accumulate. Those minerals mixed with ash from nearby erupting volcanoes, creating a unique water chemistry. As the climate warmed after the last ice age, the lake evaporated even more, exposing the rocky towers.

Violet-green swallow

Brine shrimp

Strange Shores

Temperatures **often top 120°F** (49°C) in California's Death Valley, often called the hottest place on Earth.

One reason California is nicknamed **the Golden State** is that people flooded there during the **gold rush** in the 19th century.

One out of every eight Americans **lives in California.**

1

Scientists **thought octopuses were solitary,** until they discovered massive underwater dens built with shells, which they nicknamed **"Octopolis"** and **"Octlantis."**

2

A single **octopus sucker** can **lift 35 pounds** (16 kg).

3

Octopuses have **brain cells** in **their arms.**

4

Chambered nautiluses can have as many as **90 tentacles.**

5

Because the **nautilus hasn't changed** much in **500 million years,** scientists often call it a **living fossil.**

6

The largest **giant squid** ever measured was almost 43 feet (13 m) long— that's **longer than a bus.**

7

Cuttlefish are **color-blind,** but they can **turn almost any color** to camouflage themselves.

Slippery
Facts About
Cephalopods

8

An **octopus** named Paul **correctly predicted** the winner of eight **World Cup soccer matches** in 2010.

9

The **gloomy octopus** is named for its **droopy, ghostly white eyes.**

10

The word **"cephalopod"**— a group of animals that includes **squid, octopuses, cuttlefish,** and **nautiluses**— means **"head-foot."**

Wild Facts About Parks and Preserves

1
Once the **private gardens** of five different Chinese dynasties and preserving more than **1,000 years of history,** Beihai Park in Beijing, China, was first opened for the public in 1925.

2
The world's **tallest waterfall,** Angel Falls in Venezuela's Canaima National Park is located **so deep in the forest** that visitors often choose to view it from the air.

3
With more than **400 miles** (644 km) **of caves,** Mammoth Cave National Park in Kentucky, U.S.A., protects **the longest** known **cave system** on Earth.

4
Virunga National Park, in the Democratic Republic of the Congo, safeguards **mountain gorillas,** endangered primates that can weigh **up to 400 pounds** (180 kg).

Los Glaciares National Park, Argentina

5 About half of Los Glaciares National Park in Argentina is made up of **glaciers** that **visitors can hike** across.

6 In Yellowstone National Park, U.S.A., more than **500 geysers** erupt, spewing **superhot water** that can reach temperatures higher than 200°F (93°C).

7 There are **no campsites, trails, or even roads** in the Gates of the Arctic National Park and Preserve in Alaska, U.S.A.

8 The **giant boulders** in New York City's **Central Park** were once **embedded in glaciers** that melted in New York thousands of years ago.

9 Visitors have to take either a **boat or a seaplane** to see the 19th-century **Fort Jefferson** in Dry Tortugas National Park near Key West, Florida, U.S.A., in the Gulf of Mexico.

10 **Daintree** National Park in Australia is home to **the oldest tropical rainforest** in the world.

1 After **millions of roses** are harvested in Qal'at Mgouna, Morocco, local residents take to the streets with decorated **floats** to celebrate the harvest.

2 To **celebrate winter,** marchers carrying torches at the Vulcan Victory Torchlight Parade **light up the darkness** in Saint Paul, Minnesota, U.S.A.

3 It takes **90 people** to fly the **largest balloons** at the Macy's Thanksgiving Day Parade in New York City.

4 **Thousands of dancers** from samba schools in Rio de Janeiro, Brazil, perform at the **Sambadrome** until dawn before judges and spectators during the **Rio Carnival.**

5 More than 70 different groups of revelers—or **"krewes"**—parade along the streets of New Orleans, Louisiana, U.S.A., during **Mardi Gras,** including the Rolling Elvi, people dressed like Elvis riding scooters.

6 Every inch of the floats in the annual **Rose Bowl Parade** in Pasadena, California, U.S.A., must be covered in either flowers or other **natural materials,** such as bark, seeds, or leaves.

7 In 1737, a **St. Patrick's Day parade** was held in Boston, Massachusetts, U.S.A.,—more than 160 years before Ireland held one to honor **its own patron saint.**

8 The Marksmen's Parade, in Hanover, Germany, started in the **15th century** as a showcase for people's **archery skills.**

9 In 1801, President **Thomas Jefferson** began the tradition of a **Fourth of July parade** outside the White House in Washington, D.C.

10 Every year, some **50 ships** aglow with **colored lights** parade through the harbor in Sydney, Australia, to **ring in the new year.**

Festive Facts
About
Parades

Sydney, Australia

Incredible Facts

About

Inventions

1 The inventor of the chocolate chip cookie sold her idea to Nestlé in exchange for a lifetime supply of chocolate.

2 The first **functional submarine,** used during the American Revolution, was **made of wood** and named **the Turtle** because it looked like a turtle shell.

3 Thomas Edison's laboratory was nicknamed the **Invention Factory.**

6

To ensure that no one tried to make the same product, the inventor of **pumpable hand soap** bought 100 million small pumps after his invention came out.

10

The **can opener** was invented nearly half a century after the can was introduced.

5

When he was a boy, **Benjamin Franklin** invented paddles for his hands to help him swim faster.

7

The first model of the **bicycle,** invented in 1817, didn't have any pedals.

9

Italian artist **Leonardo da Vinci** invented a scuba-like suit for underwater sneak attacks on enemy ships.

4

The temperature scale invented in 1742 by **Anders Celsius** was originally the opposite of the one we know today: 0 degrees was hot, and 100 degrees was cold.

8

The first **traffic signal** was invented in 1868 to direct horse-drawn carriages, not cars.

Green Facts
to Protect the
Planet

1

Japanese scientists discovered a strain of bacteria at a recycling plant that

eats plastics.

2

Recycling **one million cell phones** recovers about

75 pounds
(34 kg)
# of gold.

3

In Istanbul, Turkey, you get a

free subway ride

when you **recycle a plastic bottle.**

4

In one year, a **mature tree absorbs** 48 pounds (22 kg) of **carbon dioxide** from the atmosphere, which helps

clean the air.

5 At a **smoothie shop** in Portland, Oregon, U.S.A., you can **blend your own drink** by pedaling a **stationary bike** attached to a **blender.**

6 **Middle schoolers** from New York, U.S.A., designed a device that **fits on boats** to **filter out plastic** from waterways.

7 **Elephant poop** powers some of the **electricity** at **Munich Zoo** in Germany.

8 In its lifetime, one **reusable bag** can replace **600 plastic bags.**

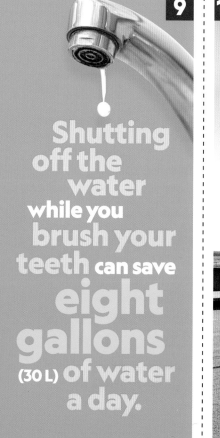

9 **Shutting off the water** while you **brush your teeth** can save **eight gallons** (30 L) of water a day.

10 **Old roof shingles** are sometimes ground up and **used to make new roads.**

51

Deep Facts About Canyons

1 Daredevil Evel Knievel **attempted to launch himself** in a **rocket** over Snake River Canyon in Idaho, U.S.A., but he failed when his parachute opened too early. (He survived.)

2 A canyon in **Death Valley National Park,** which straddles California and Nevada, U.S.A., was nicknamed **Star Wars Canyon** because parts of the Star Wars movies were filmed there.

3 The pressure at the bottom of the **Mariana Trench,** an **underwater canyon** almost seven miles (11 km) down in the Pacific Ocean, is the equivalent of **50 jumbo jets piled on top of you.**

4 The length of Valles Marineris, a **canyon on Mars,** is about the **distance between** the East Coast and the West Coast of the United States.

5 The Christmas Tree, a sparkling column covered in **crystals,** stands inside Slaughter Canyon Cave in **Carlsbad Caverns National Park** in New Mexico, U.S.A.

The
Andean condor,
found in Peru's Colca Canyon,
has a **10-foot** (3-m) **wingspan.**

6

7

Tibet's Yarlung Tsangpo Grand
Canyon is **three times deeper**
than the **Grand Canyon.**

8

The
**deepest land
canyon**
on Earth is **under the ice**
in Antarctica.

9

While some
canyons can take millions
of years to form,
narrow slot canyons
are **created instantly**
when flash floods hit soft rock.

10

Supai Village
in Arizona's **Grand Canyon**
is the only place in the United States
where mail is still delivered by
pack mule.

Grand Canyon National Park, U.S.A.

Extreme Weirdness

SUNBATHING POTATOES

WHAT Tater art

WHERE Berlin, Germany

DETAILS These aren't couch potatoes—they're beach potatoes! An artist fitted the veggies with tiny plastic sunglasses, then placed them under mini paper umbrellas on a beach-like patch of dirt. Talk about an a-peel-ing art project.

SCARY SNAKE CAKE

WHAT Reptile-shaped dessert

WHERE Kent, England

DETAILS This realistic-looking reptile is 100 percent cake. A baker created the Burmese python look-alike for her daughter's birthday party. Molding together cut-up portions of six separate cakes, it took the mom three days to create the final product. Next year's dessert might be a pie-thon.

REMOTE-CONTROLLED SUPERHERO

WHAT Superhero-shaped plane

WHERE San Diego, California, U.S.A.

DETAILS It's a bird! It's a plane! It's ... yup, it's a plane. The superhero-shaped flier—powered by a battery pack built into its "head" and operated with a remote control—took its first test flight over southern California. Made mostly of Styrofoam, the plane is just one of more than 30 pop-culture-themed fliers built by its creator. Guess you could say this is a highly cape-able aircraft.

PADDLING ON SAND

WHAT Dry river race

WHERE Alice Springs, Australia

DETAILS Sand ahoy! Regattas, or boat races, usually involve water. Not the annual Henley-on-Todd event. Contestants propel themselves with shovels from atop wheeled boogie boards, or run in groups carrying bathtubs over a dry riverbed. That's one way to make bath time more fun.

THE HANDS GO MARCHING IN

WHAT Carnaval parade

WHERE Ovar, Portugal

DETAILS Need a hand? Here are a few! Costumed paraders march down streets to celebrate Carnaval, a festival that lets people express their wild side after a couple months of winter. People often meet and walk around in kooky outfits, called masquerading, during Carnaval, which lasts about a week.

TRANSFORMER INVADES CITY

WHAT Transformer statue

WHERE London, England

DETAILS To promote the DVD release of *Transformers: Revenge of the Fallen*, a movie studio transformed the city's iconic "bendy buses" into, well, a Transformer. (A bendy bus is basically two buses attached so they can bend in the middle.) Towering 13 feet (4 m) tall, the Transformer was constructed out of real bus parts.

Massive Facts

About

Mega

1 In the 1930s, **New York City** became the **world's first** metropolitan area to have more than **10 million people.**

2 Pizzerias in **São Paulo, Brazil,** make more than **one million pizzas** a day.

3 If you added up all the **floor space** in the **shopping malls** in Jakarta, the capital of Indonesia, it would cover more than **1,000 American football fields.**

Shanghai, China

4 Located less than **10 miles** (16 km) from downtown **Cairo, Egypt,** the **Great Pyramid** towers **481 feet** (147 m) aboveground.

5 More people live in **Shanghai, China,** than in all of Chile.

Cities

6

The **ancient capital** of the Aztec, Tenochtitlan, is now the **center of Mexico City.**

7

The Shard, a skyscraper in London, England, is referred to as a **vertical city:** It has restaurants, apartments, and offices so residents never have to leave.

8

During peak hours, **thousands of people** pass through the **five crosswalks** of Shibuya Crossing in Tokyo, Japan.

9

Trains in Mumbai, India, were built to carry about **1,700 passengers,** but peak hours bring nearly **three times** that number.

10

In 2018, 33 metropolitan areas across the world had more than **10 million people—** by 2030 it's estimated there will be **43.**

57

Crawling with Bugs

Facts

1 The **Darth Vader** beetle is named for its dark, helmetlike head.

2 One species of wasp lays an egg inside a **ladybug**. The hatched larva **paralyzes** the ladybug, using it for food and protection.

3 Some moths **have ears** on their mouths.

6 The scientific name for one species of **fairy fly** is ***Tinkerbella nana***, after characters in *Peter Pan.*

Turn the page for more creepy-crawly facts!

8 Fruit flies were the **first animals launched into space.**

5 Antarctic midge larvae spend more than half of their life **frozen.**

10 The **Pacific beetle cockroach** produces a pale yellow **"milk"** that is **more nutritious** than any other kind of milk.

4 A cockroach **can live** for weeks **without its head.**

Houseflies **eat** their **own vomit.**

7

9 Mosquitoes are attracted to **smelly feet.**

59

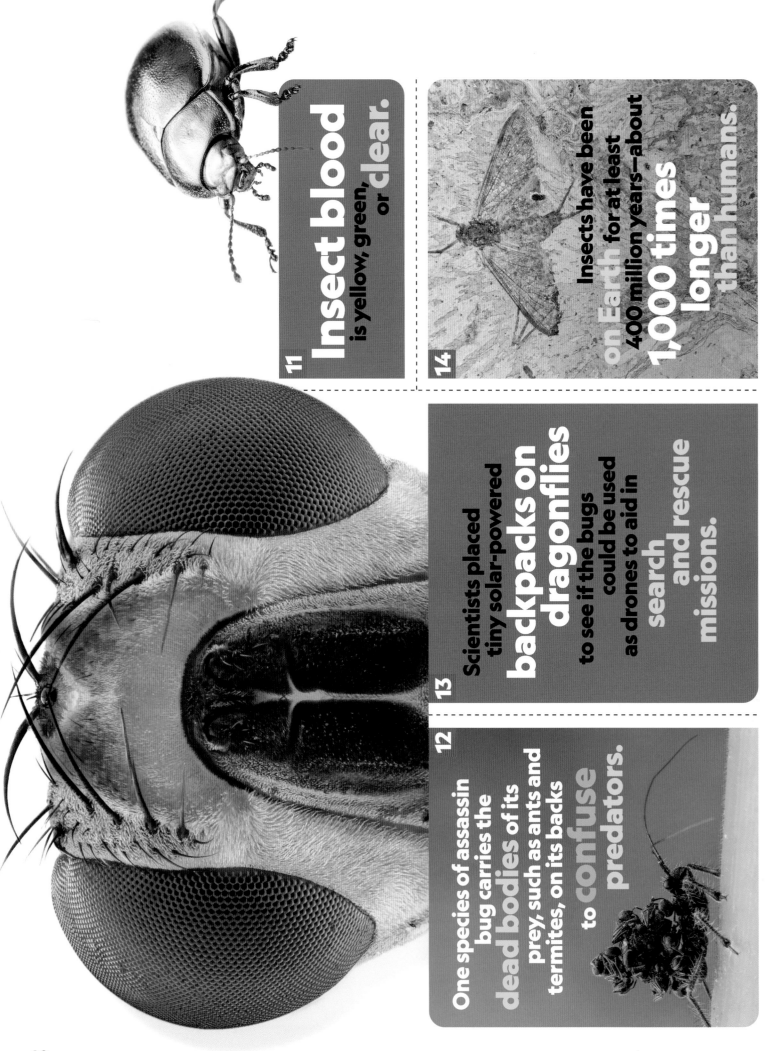

11
Insect blood
is yellow, green, or clear.

14
Insects have been on Earth for at least 400 million years—about
1,000 times longer
than humans.

13
Scientists placed tiny solar-powered
backpacks on dragonflies
to see if the bugs could be used as drones to aid in
search and rescue missions.

12
One species of assassin bug carries the **dead bodies** of its prey, such as ants and termites, on its backs to **confuse** **predators.**

15

Termites use **their own poop** to build their nests.

16

Insect **poop** is called **frass.**

17

Question Mark, Small Skipper, Red Admiral, and Painted Lady are names of types of **butterflies.**

18

Caterpillars have **12 eyes.**

19

Diving beetles can live underwater by breathing from an air bubble stored beneath their wings.

20

Most **beetles can't hear.**

61

Un-baa-lievable
Facts About
Barnyard

1 **Ducks are social—** they like to hang out in **big groups** with other ducks.

2 **Chicken moms** try to **keep their chicks away** from foods that **aren't safe** for them to eat.

3 **Pigs wag their tails** when **frustrated.**

4 **Alpacas spit** at one another when angry.

5 **Cows** chew their food for about **eight hours** a day.

Animals

6 A goat can learn its **own name** and will come when called.

7 A scientist in Pennsylvania **taught two pigs** named Hamlet and Omelette how to **play a video game** using a modified joystick.

8 Dairy cows **wag their tails** when they are **brushed,** which researchers think indicates happiness.

9 Chickens and ostriches are the **closest living relatives** to *Tyrannosaurus rex.*

10 Sheep can **solve mazes** and remember the path at least **six weeks later.**

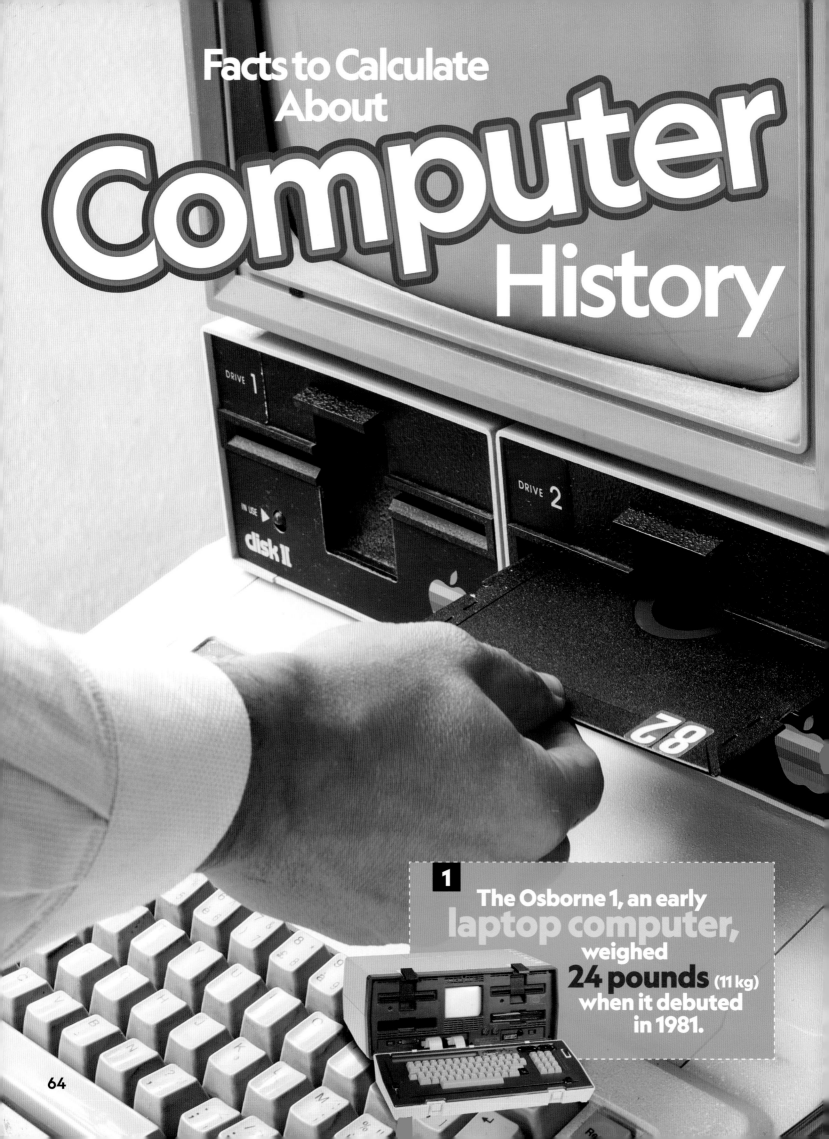

Facts to Calculate About Computer History

1

The Osborne 1, an early **laptop computer,** weighed **24 pounds** (11 kg) when it debuted in 1981.

2 In 2015, researchers at the University of Michigan in the United States created the **Micro Mote,** a computer so small that nearly **150** could fit into a thimble.

3 President **Bill Clinton** became the first American president to **send an email—** a message **to astronaut John Glenn** while he was on the space shuttle.

4 In **the 1960s,** J. C. R. Licklider, a scientist at the Massachusetts Institute of Technology, had an idea for a **global network** of computers he called the **Galactic Network.**

5 In the late 1800s, **looms were programmed** to read **punched cards** that contained instructions on how to make cloth.

6 In the 1820s, English mathematician **Charles Babbage** imagined a type of **calculator** powered by a steam engine—when built, it had **8,000 parts** and was eight feet (2.4 m) tall.

7 In 1946, in a **science fiction** short story called "A Logic Named Joe," the world was connected by a **network of computers.**

8 On October 29, 1969, the internet's **first message** was sent between two computers at two California universities— **the message was "lo,"** as the system **crashed** before the full word **"login"** could be sent.

9 Nicknamed the **"fuzzball,"** an early **internet router** developed in the 1970s could send **300 packets** of information a second. (Routers today can handle more than one billion a second.)

10 **Tim Berners-Lee,** the inventor of the **World Wide Web,** was **knighted** by Queen Elizabeth II.

65

Freewheeling
Facts About
Bicycles

1 Considered by many as the birthplace of **bikepacking,** the nearly 3,000-mile (4,828-km)-long **Great Divide Mountain Bike Route** follows the Rocky Mountains from Jasper, Alberta, Canada, to Antelope Wells, New Mexico, U.S.A.

2 A man in Lithuania created a **3,053-pound** (1,385-kg) **rideable bicycle—** the **heaviest** in the world.

3 Before they built airplanes, **Orville and Wilbur Wright sold bikes** they made in their Dayton, Ohio, U.S.A., shop.

4 The **leader** of the **Tour de France** wears a **yellow jersey** because the newspaper that first sponsored the race was printed on yellow paper.

Bicycle motocross

(BMX), a sport in which riders **race bicycles around a track,** became an Olympic sport in the 2008 Summer Games.

5 Nicknamed **boneshakers,** bikes made of iron and wood gave people a **very bumpy** ride in the 1860s.

6

8 At the Indy Crit Bicycle Parade in Indianapolis, Indiana, U.S.A., you can watch **brass and polka bands** play while they ride, as well as bicyclists on **"costumed" bikes.**

7 Karl von Drais, an **early bicyclemaker,** realized that people **could balance** while moving forward on two wheels by **watching ice skaters.**

10 In 2016, people in the Netherlands traveled more than **9.6 billion miles** (15.5 billion km) by bike—that's more than **20,200 trips to the moon** and back!

9 Astronauts on the **International Space Station** can still **ride a bike—** it's known as the Cycle Ergometer with Vibration Isolation and Stabilization System (CEVIS).

Facts About Breakfast Foods
to Wake You Up

1 **Canada** has more **doughnut shops** per person than **any other country.**

2

Competitors at a **pancake race** in Olney, England, **wear an apron** and run **holding a frying pan** containing a hot pancake.

3 More than **half of Americans** **eat cereal** for breakfast, a survey found.

The word **"bagel"** comes from a German word meaning **"bracelet."**

4

Coffee beans aren't beans— they're **seeds.**

5

6

The cofounder of Nike used a **waffle iron** to make the company's first pair of **Waffle Trainer** running shoes.

7

It takes **40 gallons** (151 L) of **maple tree sap** to make one gallon (3.8 L) of **maple syrup.**

8

The **largest pancake** ever made was **49 feet** (15 m) **wide.**

9

If an egg **spins easily** on a flat surface, **it's cooked,** but if it **wobbles, it's raw.**

10

It takes about **three oranges** to make **one glass** of orange juice.

Extraordinary
Facts About the
Future

1

Fashion designers are looking to design clothes that **"grow"** as kids grow, using stretchy material and pleats that unfold.

2

To reduce pollution and the cost of transporting food, cities may soon have **floating farms** in nearby bodies of water.

3

Drones may soon replace drivers for **delivering** everything from packages to **pizza.**

4

Plans are underway for people to travel through **underground tubes** in pods that cruise **faster than a jet.**

5

Plastic
may soon be made from
biodegradable
materials such as
algae or fish skin.

6

Future astronauts
on their journey to Mars
may grow
algae-based food
that tastes like caviar.

7

"Smart" contact lenses
will not only correct vision but will also
display
information like
directions and sports scores.

8

Instead of
fitness bracelets,
people may soon
wear clothing
made with
"smart fabric"
that measures
heart rates.

9

Boeing has plans to make
a **hypersonic airplane**
that can fly from
New York City to
London in two hours.
(It currently takes
seven hours.)

10

Instead of
a physician or nurse,
robots
will take your
temperature
and blood pressure
at the doctor's office.

What's the Difference?

PORCUPINE VS. HEDGEHOG

Porcupines and hedgehogs are not closely related, but their pokey form of protection makes them equally eye-catching. Porcupines are about three feet (1 m) long (not including the tail), and they live on every continent except Australia and Antarctica. These herbivores spend much of their time in trees eating fruits and plants. They have as many as 30,000 quills, which typically lay flat on their backs, but when the animal is threatened, they stand straight up. The quills detach easily and are painful to the predator that gets poked! Hedgehogs are only five to 12 inches (13 to 31 cm) long and spend their time in hedges and under logs, looking for insects, worms, snails, and frogs to eat. They aren't quite as widespread as porcupines: They live in the wild in Europe, Asia, Africa, and New Zealand. Hedgehogs have stiff, sharp spines that they use as protection. When threatened, hedgehogs roll up into a spiky ball to protect their soft bellies. Hedgehog spines don't easily detach.

Hedgehog

Lacrosse

VEIN VS. ARTERY

Arteries carry blood away from the heart, and veins carry it back again. But it's not that simple. There are two types of circulation in your body: systemic circulation—blood travels all around your body—and pulmonary circulation—blood travels from the heart to the lungs and back to the heart again. ("Pulmonary" just means something related to the lungs.) The pulmonary artery carries blood away from the heart to the lungs so the blood can become rich in oxygen, and then pulmonary veins bring the oxygen-rich blood to the heart, which pumps it around the body. Then super-small branches of blood vessels called capillaries link arteries and veins. That's when the veins take over, carrying the blood back to the heart, where the cycle starts all over again.

NECTAR VS. POLLEN

Have you heard the expression "busy as a bee"? Why are bees so busy? The answer has to do with nectar and pollen. Bees visit flowers and slurp up plant nectar, a sugary liquid. The nectar is held in a special "honey" stomach to take back to the hive. There, bees pass the nectar from mouth to mouth in a process that turns it into honey. When bees visit flowers, they also brush up against pollen grains, which stick to their bodies. Some of this pollen falls off when they fly to other plants, which is how the plants reproduce. As for humans, pollen might make us sneeze, but honey makes us happy!

FIELD HOCKEY VS. LACROSSE

Lacrosse and field hockey are both played on a field with players using sticks to pass a small ball. But that's where the similarities end between these two sports, which have been played in various parts of the world for centuries. Field hockey has 11 players on each team who move the ball on the ground using a stick rounded at the end. The goal is to pass and shoot the ball into the opponent's goal. Think of it as soccer, but you use a stick instead of your feet. In lacrosse, a team of 10 players throws and catches the ball in the air with sticks that have a net on the end. Lacrosse is more of a contact sport than field hockey, and players wear more protective gear, including pads and face masks. Lacrosse does have the same objective as field hockey: Score more goals than the other team.

ROBOT VS. ANDROID

Here's the difference between a robot and an android: An android is a robot, but a robot isn't necessarily an android. Confused? Let's break it down. A robot is a machine that can carry out tasks written into a computer program. Even though it can execute a task on its own, a human has to program what it does. For example, the self-cleaning robots that zip around the living room sweeping up pet hair are robots. Androids are robots and are programmed just like other robots, but they look like humans. This is the stuff of science fiction that's becoming reality. In Japan, an android named Erica works as a newscaster. She looks like a person and even talks and moves like her human counterpart. While robots and androids seem futuristic, similar ideas have been around for a long time. In 1495, Italian artist and inventor Leonardo da Vinci created an armored suit that moved with the help of pulleys, cables, gears, and wheels. It could even wave its sword and open and close its mouth!

Android

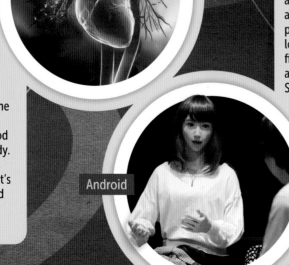

Glacier

Iceberg

GLACIER VS. ICEBERG

Glaciers and icebergs are both made of ice, but if you had to spend the night on one, a glacier is the safer bet! That's because icebergs form when parts of a glacier break off and start to float in the ocean or a lake. This is known as calving. Glaciers form in areas where masses of snow turn into ice over time, so they are always on land. If you were on an iceberg, you'd travel along with the water currents. Since the chunks that break off glaciers come in all different sizes, scientists use the word "icebergs" to refer to pieces at least 16 feet (5 m) across.

1
Impalas, a type of antelope, can **jump 10 feet** (3 m) high—that's the height of an elephant.

2
A **giraffe's eye** is as big as a **Ping-Pong ball.**

3
A black rhino's **horns grow three inches** (8 cm) every year.

4
A **zebra's skin is black** under its striped coat.

5
As many as 1.5 million **wildebeest** migrate 620 miles (1,000 km) across Africa's Serengeti each year in search of food.

A dik-dik, the **smallest** Serengeti antelope, is the size of a **miniature poodle.**

6

7 **Leopards** get most of the **water they need** from eating **their prey.**

8 A **lion's heels** don't **touch the ground** when it walks.

9 Scientists can tell **how old** a **hyena** is and **where it ranks** in its clan based on the sound of its "laugh."

10 With their **strong jaws, hippos** can **snap a canoe** in half with one bite.

Surprising Facts About Animals on the Serengeti

1 **Crocodiles survived** the extinction event that **killed the dinosaurs.**

2 A **brown bear** is an **apex predator** that weighs as much as **800 pounds** (363 kg), but much of its diet consists of nuts, berries, leaves, and roots.

3 About as **big as a dinner plate,** the Goliath birdeater is large enough to **eat birds,** but it usually eats mice, frogs, and lizards.

4 **Snow leopards can leap** as far as 50 feet (15 m), taking down prey **three times** their own weight.

5 The **tongue** of a blue whale, which helps it swallow millions of shrimplike animals called krill each day, **can weigh** as much as **an elephant.**

6 A single gray wolf can eat **20 pounds** (9 kg) **of meat** in one sitting— that's like you eating **80 hamburgers.**

7 After a chase, **a cheetah needs** a half hour to **catch its breath** before it can eat.

8 The **black king snake** is **resistant to the toxins** of venomous snakes and often **preys on rattlesnakes,** copperheads, and cottonmouths.

9 Frigate birds hunt over the ocean but will **drown if they get wet,** so they have to **catch flying fish** or steal fish caught by other seabirds.

10 At only about three pounds (1.4 kg), the **fennec fox** is about the size of a kitten but has giant six-inch (15-cm) ears it uses to **hear prey** underneath the sand.

Powerful Predator Facts

1 Two **giant concrete hands** support a nearly 500-foot (152-m)-tall **walking bridge** outside Da Nang, Vietnam.

2 **Giant tree roots** have grown into the 12th-century Ta Prohm Temple, a former monastery in Angkor Wat, Cambodia, **merging buildings** and **forest.**

3 It took about **20,000 workers** to build India's **Taj Mahal** in the 1600s.

4 Paddlers **race boats** fashioned with **dragon heads** and tails in Hong Kong's annual Dragon Boat Festival.

5 When building China's **Great Wall,** workers added **sticky rice** to the mortar to increase its strength.

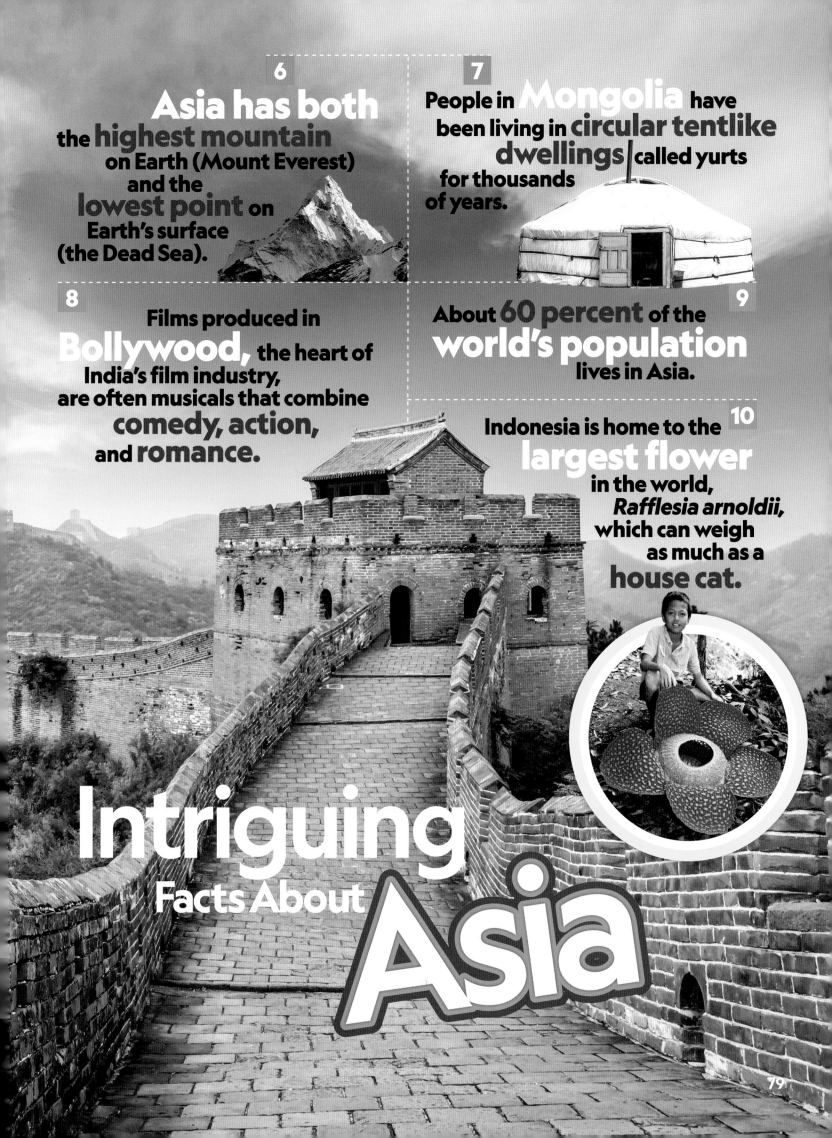

6

Asia has both the **highest mountain** on Earth (Mount Everest) and the **lowest point** on Earth's surface (the Dead Sea).

7

People in **Mongolia** have been living in **circular tentlike dwellings** called yurts for thousands of years.

8

Films produced in **Bollywood,** the heart of India's film industry, are often musicals that combine **comedy, action,** and **romance.**

9

About **60 percent** of the **world's population** lives in Asia.

10

Indonesia is home to the **largest flower** in the world, *Rafflesia arnoldii,* which can weigh as much as a **house cat.**

Intriguing
Facts About
Asia

Open These Facts About Shells

1

The **whooshing sound** you hear when you put a seashell to your ear isn't the ocean; it's the shell making the **noises around you** louder.

2

Scientists found **carvings on shells** that *Homo erectus,* an ancestor of modern humans, may have made half a million years ago.

3

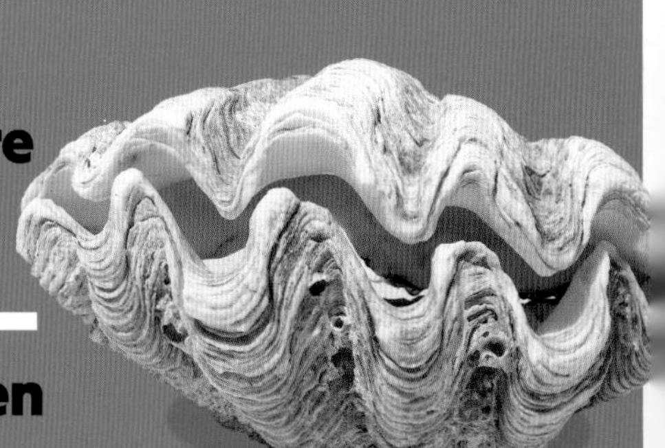

Most seashells are **right-handed—** they open to the right.

4

Oysters grow on each other, creating reefs that form a community for many types of marine animals.

3,000 years ago in Peru, people used **seashells** as **musical instruments.**

5 When some hermit crabs **smell a dead hermit crab,** they scurry to the site to **eat the carcass—** and one might even **move into the shell.**

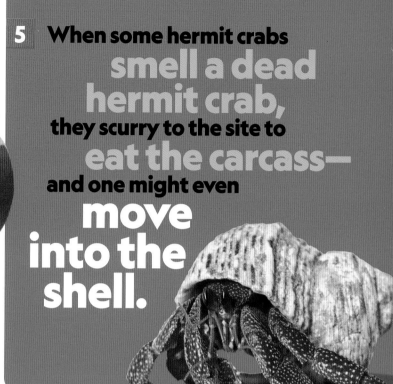

6

Most seashells are the **outer skeletons** of animals known as **mollusks.**

8

7 When a seashell **has a hole in it,** that usually means a **predator drilled** into it to eat the animal inside.

9 **Thousands of years ago** in China and Africa, seashells were **used as money.**

10 Female argonaut octopuses **build delicate, paperlike shells** to lay their eggs in.

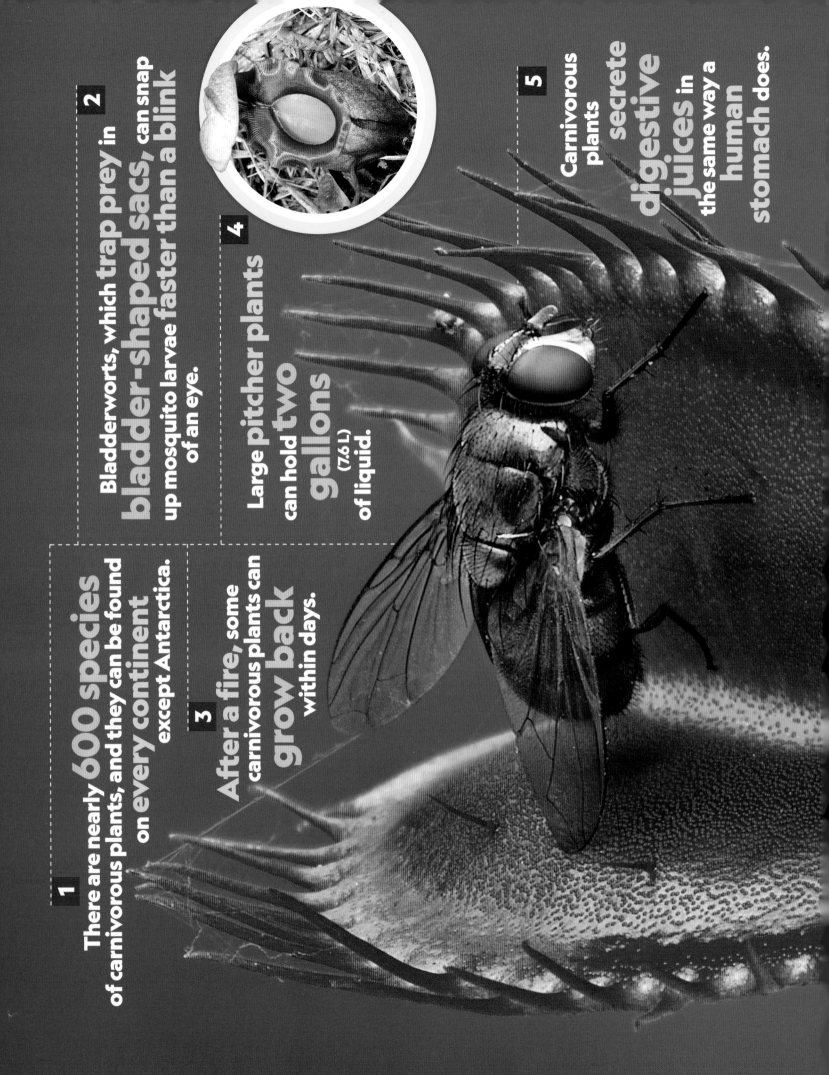

1

There are nearly **600 species** of carnivorous plants, and they can be found on every continent except Antarctica.

2

Bladderworts, which trap prey in **bladder-shaped sacs,** can snap up mosquito larvae faster than a blink of an eye.

3

After a fire, some carnivorous plants can **grow back** within days.

4

Large pitcher plants can hold **two gallons** (7.6 L) of liquid.

5

Carnivorous plants secrete **digestive juices** in the same way a human stomach does.

Meaty Facts About Carnivorous Plants

6
A sundew plant in Australia uses **sticky tentacles** to capture insects.

7
Venus flytraps digest ants and spiders, don't consume bees, but they **don't consume bees,** which pollinate them.

8
Small rats and tree shrews on the island of Borneo slurp nectar from the lids of pitcher plants and then "feed" the plant by **pooping into its pitcher.**

9
Most pitcher plants have two kinds of pitchers— ones low to the ground to catch crawling insects and ones higher up to catch **flying ones.**

10
Researchers found that pitcher plants in Canada's Algonquin Provincial Park **digest small salamanders**— the first time a North American carnivorous plant was found to snack on amphibians.

Venus flytrap

83

When on the ground, sloths move by digging their front claws into the ground and **dragging themselves** along.

1

2
Sloths must **come down** out of the trees— and **risk being eaten** by a predator—to poop on the **ground.**

3
The three-toed sloth— the **slowest moving** mammal on Earth—is so still that predators like the harpy eagle have trouble spotting it.

4
A sloth spends almost **its entire life** hanging **upside down.**

5
The **two-toed sloth has three toes** on its back legs (but two fingers on its front ones).

6
About 10,000 years ago, a **sloth as big as an elephant** lived in what is now **South America.**

7 A sloth can **turn its head** almost **all the way around.**

8 Sloths poop about once a week.

9 The fur of a three-toed sloth is **full of insects,** and birds like the brown jay swoop down to **eat the bugs** from it.

10 Sloths are **excellent swimmers** and can **hold their breath** underwater for up to **40 minutes.**

Sloth
Facts to Hang Out With

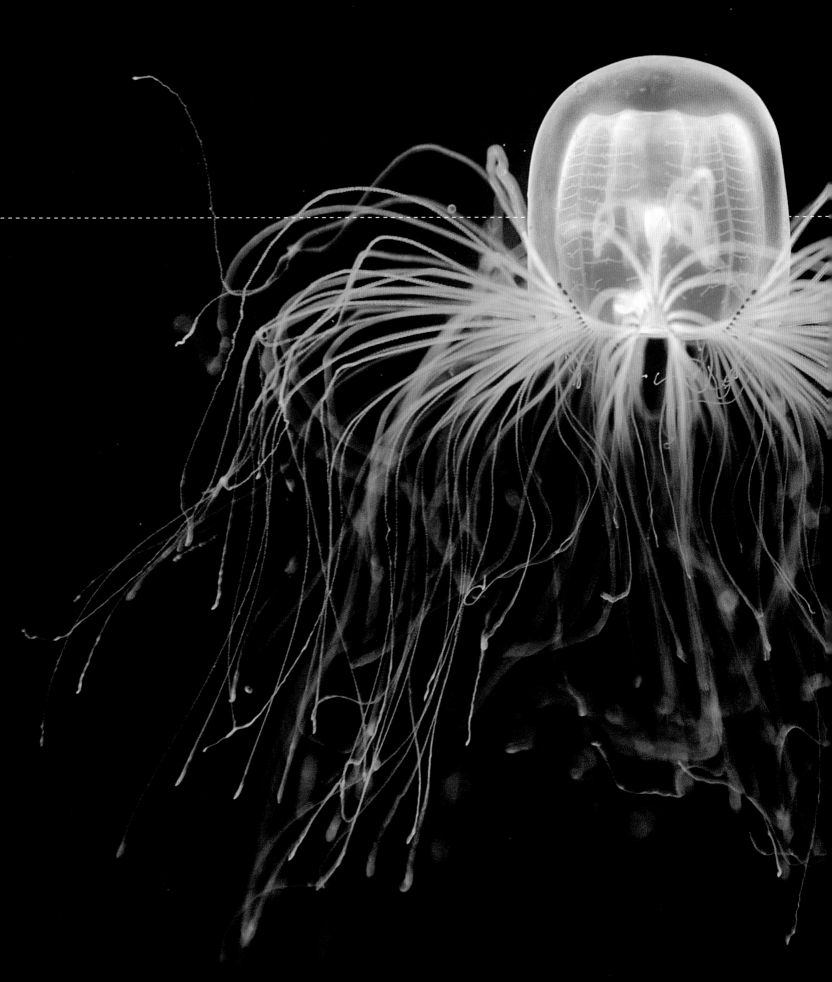

Unless it gets sick or is eaten, the immortal jellyfish cannot die.

When **threatened,** it can turn back into a polyp, its earliest stage of life, and **begin** the growth process **all over again.**

The Baikal seal, found only in Siberia's Lake Baikal, has **big, bulging eyes** to help it find prey in the **world's deepest lake.**

1

2

Almost **70 percent of Earth's freshwater** is found in **ice caps** and **glaciers.**

3 **The Nile River—** the world's longest river— originates in streams in East Africa and flows more than **4,000 miles** (6,400 km) **northward before emptying into the Mediterranean Sea.**

Splashy
Facts About
Rivers and Lakes

Melissani Lake

4
Every day, some **100 million gallons** (379 million L) **of water flow from the** spring at **Manatee Springs State Park, in Florida, U.S.A., into the Suwannee River.**

5
NASA scientists calculated that **the amount of water** in the reservoir of the **Three Gorges Dam** on China's Yangtze River **lengthened** a day on Earth by .06 microseconds.

6
You can see **262 feet** (80 m) into New Zealand's **Blue Lake,** which is why it's known as the **clearest lake** in the world.

7
In 2007, it took Martin Strel **66 days to swim** the full length of the **Amazon River** in South America.

8
At 12,500 feet (3,810 m) in elevation, **Lake Titicaca** in South America is the **world's highest lake** that large boats can navigate.

9
The European country of **Finland** has nearly **188,000 lakes.**

10
In 1953, an **earthquake** on the Greek island of Kefalonia caused **rocks to collapse, revealing a lake** in Melissani Cave.

Elemental
Facts About
Elements

1

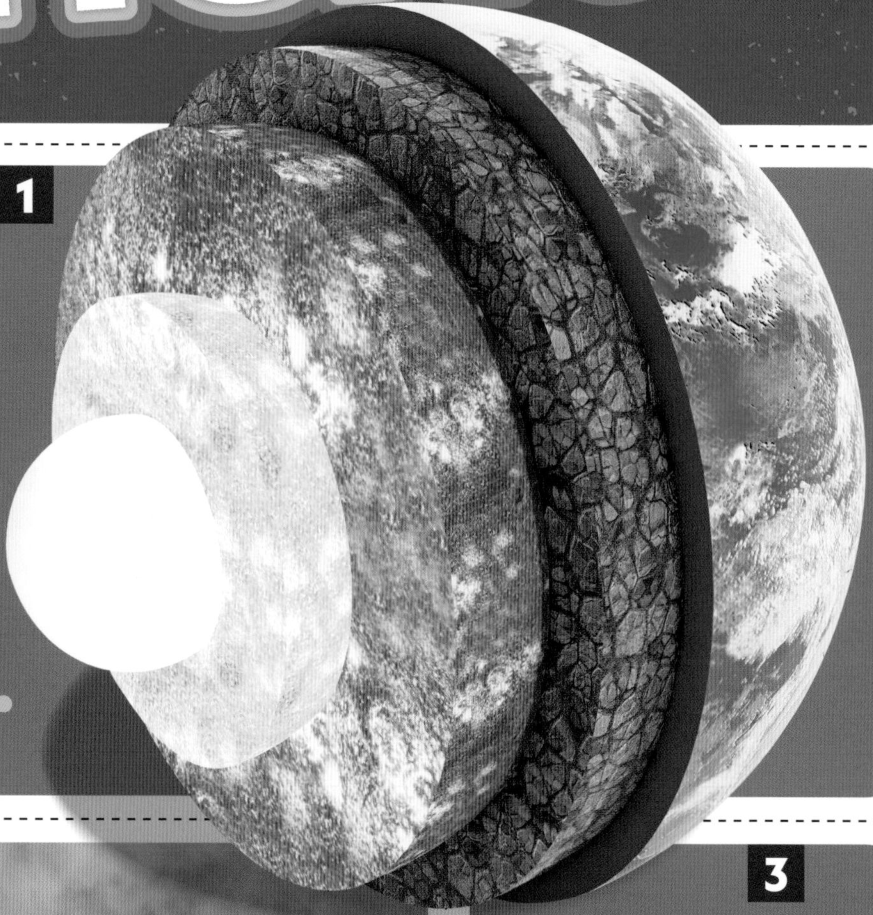

Earth's core
is a
white-
hot solid
ball
made mostly of iron.

2

Helium
balloons
float because helium is
lighter
than air.

3

The
periodic
table of
elements
has been
used to
predict the
existence
of elements
before
they were
discovered.

Europium, which **glows red** under ultraviolet light, is used in European paper money to help **prevent forgery.**

Every living thing on Earth contains **carbon.**

4

5

Ancient Romans paid their soldiers in sodium chloride, also known as **table salt.**

6

7

Helium was used in the **first rockets** that carried astronauts into space and in the **lunar lander** that put the first humans **on the moon.**

8

Russian scientist Dmitri Mendeleev created the **periodic table of elements,** which he claimed he saw in a **dream.**

9

10

Sodium explodes if you toss it into **water.**

Scientists are looking to **the Arctic, the deep sea, asteroids,** and **the moon** to **mine for elements.**

More than three million lights, which **change patterns** every minute, illuminate a floating 278-foot (85-m)-tall metal tree in the Rodrigo de Freitas Lagoon in Rio de Janeiro, Brazil.

1

2

During the **summer solstice** in Latvia, people raise poles topped with **burning barrels** to symbolize the **victory of light** over darkness.

3

In 1880, American inventor Thomas Edison created the **first strand** of **electric lights.**

4

In 2015, a 56-foot (17-m)-tall **giant holiday ball** was strung with 23,120 lights in **Moscow,** Russia.

Some **holiday lights** can be **seen from outer space.**

5

6

Since 1951, **the lighting** of the Christmas tree at **Rockefeller Center** in New York City has been **broadcast live** all over the world.

Holiday

Facts to
Light Up Your Day

7 The 30-foot (9-m)-high **National Menorah** in Washington, D.C., is lit from a **cherry picker.**

8 In 1903, when people could first buy **strings of Christmas lights,** they had to **hire an electrician** to set them up.

9 During **Diwali,** the festival of lights, people in the town of Ayodhya, India, lit more than **900,000 oil lamps—** a world record.

10 At a winter **light festival** in Kanagawa, Japan, the **hills are covered** with some six million **LED lights.**

Could a new discovery help solve this ancient puzzle?

Dazzling rays from the sun burst through a strange ring of stones set on a grassy field. Some of these rocks rise 20 feet (6 m) in the air. Others lie scattered on the ground. This huge monument, called Stonehenge, has towered above England's Salisbury Plain for thousands of years—but it's still one of the world's biggest mysteries.

THE UNEXPLAINED

For centuries people have tried to unlock Stonehenge's secrets. A legend from the 12th century claimed that giants placed the monument on a mountain in Ireland, then a wizard named Merlin magically moved the stone circle to England. Other theories have suggested that migrants from continental Europe built the site as an astronomical observatory or as a temple to the sun and moon gods. No theories have been proved. But a new find may provide more information about the builders of Stonehenge and could help explain why the monument was constructed in this region.

HUNTING FOR CLUES

Many scientists had guessed that the builders of Stonehenge were the first to settle the area some 5,000 years ago, around 3000 B.C., when construction on the site began. A recent excavation is making people rethink this idea. While digging around a spring about a mile and a half (2.4 km) from Stonehenge, archaeologist David Jacques and his team uncovered hundreds of bones belonging to aurochs—a species of cattle twice the size of a modern-day bull that thrived in ancient times. In fact the site, known as Vespasian's Camp, held the largest collection of auroch bones ever found in Europe. That suggests that the spring was a pit stop along an auroch migration route where the animals drank water. The team also unearthed 31,000 flints, a stone tool used for hunting. "We started to wonder if the area was also a hunting ground and feasting site for ancient people," Jacques says. "Just one auroch could've fed a hundred people, so the place would've been a big draw." One of the excavated flints was made from a type of rock found some 75 miles (121 km) to the west. "This means people may have traveled from all over to hunt here," Jacques says. The animal bones and tools date back to 7500 B.C. The age of the artifacts caused Jacques to conclude that people moved to the region around 9,500 years ago—4,500 years earlier than what some had thought—to hunt auroch. And he thinks descendants of these settlers assembled the mysterious stone ring.

STONEHENGE, THE PREQUEL?

The first settlers may have even had their own early version of Stonehenge. Jacques thinks they set up a group of wooden posts 650 feet from where Stonehenge now stands. At least 8,500 years old, the posts were found during construction of a parking lot. This wooden monument may have been a tribute to the settlers' ancestors. Jacques and other scientists will keep digging for more clues that just might solve the mysteries of Stonehenge once and for all. But for now its story isn't written in stone.

STONE ZONE

It's too bad a wizard didn't help build Stonehenge. It was made with 4,000-pound bluestone rocks, and 50,000-pound sarsen stones. Funded in part by the National Geographic Society, archaeologist Mike Parker Pearson is studying where the stones originated and how people moved them to their current spot without wheeled vehicles. The sarsens were possibly hauled in on big wooden sleds from 20 miles away. The bluestones were traced to rock outcrops 140 miles away in present-day Wales, in the United Kingdom. Parker Pearson thinks they could have been dragged on sleds to a waterway and then floated on rafts to the building site. Parker Pearson is also investigating if the bluestones were first set up as circular monuments in Wales, then dismantled and taken to Salisbury Plain. One thing's for sure: The builders must've had rock-hard muscles.

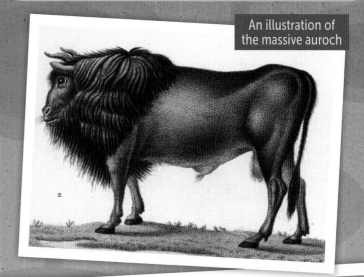

An illustration of the massive auroch

The Secrets of Stonehenge

1

Only about **8 to 10 percent** of people have **blue eyes.**

2

Dust in Earth's atmosphere can **make the moon look blue.**

3

A **"blue moon"** doesn't mean the moon is blue—it's the **second full moon** to appear in a **single month.**

Brilliant
Facts About
the Color
Blue

7

The **bluebottle jellyfish,** also known as the Portuguese man-of-war, is not a single animal but a colony of four kinds of creatures.

4

Blue jay feathers are actually brown, but they look blue because light scatters when it hits the feathers and only blue is reflected back to your eyes.

5

Tiny **bioluminescent** organisms nicknamed **sea sparkles** make the water surrounding Taiwan's Matsu Islands glow **blue.**

6

According to some surveys, blue is the **most popular color** in the world.

8

Some scientists think that people in ancient cultures, such as the Greeks, **couldn't see** the color blue.

9

Blue is the **rarest** occurring color **found in nature.**

10

In 1995, people voted for blue—instead of pink or purple—as **the new color** for **M&M's.**

Snack on

Tasty Facts About

Cookies

1 In the United States, the first week in December is National **Cookie Cutter** Week.

4 In 2018, Nabisco redesigned its **animal crackers box** to show the animals free in the wild rather than in cages.

3 A bakery in North Carolina, U.S.A., once baked a chocolate chip cookie that was **102 feet** (31 m) across—that's about the length of two semitrailers.

2 In Asia, Oreos come in **green tea** flavor.

7

Cookie Monster's cookies are actually rice cakes painted to look like cookies.

6

Because of sugar, butter, and flour shortages during World War II, **Girl Scouts sold calendars** rather than cookies to raise money.

8

A bakery in Cork, Ireland, once baked **4,695 cookies** in one hour.

10

The **first chocolate chip cookie was the size of a quarter.**

5

Fortune cookies were **invented in Japan,** not China.

9

Boxes of animal crackers were originally intended as **Christmas tree ornaments.**

99

Nighttime Facts About
Nocturnal Animals

1

Barn owls are able to **swoop up prey** silently because the **soft edges** of their wings muffle sound.

2

Moonrats, a type of mammal, **mark their territory** at night with a scent that smells like **rotten garlic.**

3

A tarsier's **eyeball** is **bigger than** its **brain;** it uses its big peepers to see at night.

4

Whiskers on a fox's legs help it feel its way **through tall grass** at night.

7

The tube-lipped nectar bat, which feeds on flower nectar at night, has a tongue that's longer than its body.

5

To escape predators, an opossum sometimes plays "dead," flopping on its side with its tongue out.

8

Some scientists think a raccoon's "mask" marking helps reduce glare so it can see better at night.

6

Wolverines, which hunt at night, can smell hibernating prey buried 20 feet (6 m) under snow.

9

After sunset, an aardvark hunts and licks up some 50,000 ants with its sticky tongue.

10

Bush babies make a call that sounds like a human baby crying.

1

Dung beetles eat poop from mammals and can carry a ball of dung that's 50 times their own weight.

2

Microscopic mites live in pores on your face, and they come out when you're asleep.

3

Wood rats pee all over their nests, which helps preserve them.

Funky Facts

That Will
Gross You Out

4 Burrowing beetles **lay their eggs** near a **dead animal,** such as a mouse or a snake, so that the newly hatched baby beetles will have a **ready meal.**

5 Owls often **regurgitate** their prey's **teeth and bones** because they **can't digest** them.

6 Pacific hagfish **burrow inside** the body of a **dead animal** to eat it from the **inside out.**

7 The common eider, a kind of duck, **covers its eggs** in its **own droppings** when startled from its nest, which might keep predators away.

8 One species of beaded lacewing **stuns and kills** its prey **by tooting** on it.

9 A bombardier beetle shoots **toxins from its bottom** to protect itself.

10 The **tongue-eating louse** **slurps blood** from a fish's tongue until the tongue withers away, and then the louse becomes the **new "tongue"** in the fish's mouth.

1 Pirates rarely **buried treasure—** either because they **preferred to spend it** or because the loot was food or clothing.

2 An English merchant buried **six bags of silver** (he had bought the loot from pirates) in the York River in Virginia, U.S.A., but was **turned in** before he could **retrieve the riches.**

3 A 1692 earthquake and tsunami **nearly destroyed** the **pirate stronghold** of Port Royal, Jamaica— the **sea swallowed** about two-thirds of the city.

4 **Madame Ching Shih,** a powerful early-19th-century **Chinese pirate,** commanded some **80,000 men.** (Blackbeard commanded about 300.)

Pirate

Facts That Will Shiver Your Timbers

5 Pirate pair **Rachel and George Wall** targeted ships off the New Hampshire, U.S.A., coast by pretending to need help.

6 Pirates in early America called their coins **"pieces of eight,"** which were Spanish silver dollar coins that often had an "8" stamped on them.

7 A **black flag** meant that pirates would spare the lives of sailors who surrendered, but a red flag signaled no mercy.

8 Legend holds that Blackbeard's **headless body** was buried on Ocracoke Island on the Outer Banks of North Carolina, U.S.A., after he was killed there in November 1718.

9 Pirates followed a **strict code of laws** on board—and rule breakers could be severely punished.

10 It's unlikely that pirates ever made people **walk the plank.**

Extreme Weirdness

ATTACK OF THE FEATHERS

WHAT International Pillow Fight Day

WHERE Around the world

DETAILS Feathers were flying as a massive crowd bopped each other with pillows. More than a hundred cities participated in the event, which was held to encourage people to get off their rumps and play.

WOMAN TURNS INTO SODA MACHINE

WHAT Human vending machine

WHERE Tokyo, Japan

DETAILS How do you hide if a monster is chasing you down the street? Disguise yourself as a vending machine, of course! Fashion designer Aya Tsukioka created a layered skirt that doubles as a hiding place. When you lift the top layer in front of your head, it looks like a soda machine to hide behind. Let's just hope the monster doesn't crave a bubbly beverage.

BLINGED-OUT BENZ

WHAT Crystal-covered cars

WHERE Chiba, Japan

DETAILS Someone went a little crazy with the glue gun. A luxury auto company embellished two cars—one painted silver and the other gold—with 300,000 crystals. Each. The cars, worth about a million dollars apiece, were on display at the Tokyo Auto Salon. Pedestrians, get out your sunglasses!

PIE IN THE SKY

WHAT Sky-high restaurant

WHERE Brussels, Belgium

DETAILS Whatever you do, don't drop your silverware. Dinner in the Sky lifts its diners, table, and waitstaff about 160 feet into the air for a meal. Guests are strapped to their seats the entire time. Although based in Belgium, the restaurant can be driven almost anywhere. Next stop, space?

FROZEN FOOD

WHAT Chilly chili-eating contest

WHERE Hangzhou, China

DETAILS Hot or cold? How about both! Participants in this contest tried to eat as many hot peppers as they could—while sitting in barrels of ice water. The winner ate 62 peppers in three minutes and earned a gold bar as his trophy. Bet he'll never order hot sauce again.

STRAW MAN

WHAT Straw bears

WHERE Heldra, Germany

DETAILS Somebody went overboard with their winter coat. In colder months, some Germans have a tradition of wearing outfits made of straw while attending seasonal festivals. These "straw bears" date back to an old belief that the outfits would scare winter away. All this guy needs is a straw scarf.

1

The **closest black hole** to Earth is about **1,000 light-years** away.

2

A black hole's **gravity** is **so strong it pulls in** nearby material— including **stars**—and **"eats" it.**

3

Supermassive black holes are more than a **million times larger** than the sun.

4

It took **eight telescopes** working around the world **at the same time** to **capture the first image** of a black hole in 2019.

5

Black holes eventually **evaporate** until there is **nothing left.**

6

Black holes are the **only objects** in **the universe** that can **trap light.**

7

If you **fell into** a black hole, you'd stretch **like a noodle**— which scientists call **spaghettification.**

8

When two **black holes collide, they merge** to make an **even bigger** black hole.

9

A **black hole** usually forms when a **massive star collapses** in on itself.

10

Our sun isn't big enough to become a black hole.

Bright Facts
About
Black Holes

Check Into
These Facts About Cool
Hotels

1 At North Shire in England, visitors can stay in the **Dorm Room Cottage,** which is modeled on the **Gryffindor** dormitories from the Harry Potter series.

2 At the Cristalino Lodge in Brazil, you can view **birds and monkeys** in the Amazon **rainforest canopy** from two 165-foot (50-m)-tall towers.

3 Guests at two hotels in Austria can **sleep outside** in repurposed concrete **drainage pipes.**

4

The Henn na Hotel in Tokyo, Japan, employs a **robotic dinosaur** to **greet guests** and check them into their rooms.

5

Every April, you can view the **northern lights** from **heated igloo pods** at the North Pole.

6

You can stay overnight in an abandoned **lighthouse** in Long Island Sound with views of **New York City's** skyline.

7

Guests at the Dog Bark Park Inn in Cottonwood, Idaho, U.S.A., can sleep in the "muzzle" of a **two-story-tall house** that looks like a **beagle.**

8

Hotel owners transformed a 1965 Boeing **727 airplane** into a **two-bedroom lodge** that looks like it's flying out of a Costa Rican **rainforest.**

9

At a hotel overlooking Capertee Valley in Australia, guests stay in secluded, **see-through bubble** tents perfect for stargazing.

10

Canada's Hotel de Glace **features rooms and beds carved out of ice.**

111

Owls

1

Owls can't move their eyes.

2

Soaring at the cruising altitude of a commercial airplane, the Ruppell's griffon vulture is the **highest-flying bird** in the world.

High-Flying
Facts About
Birds of Prey

3 The bald eagle's call is more of a chuckle than a mighty cry, so in movies it's dubbed over with the piercing screech of a red-tailed hawk.

4 The peregrine falcon is the fastest animal in the world, with a top speed of 200 miles an hour (322 km/h), three times faster than a cheetah.

5 From the air, kestrels can spot lines of urine their prey left on the ground.

6 Vultures can eat meat so rotten it would make other animals sick.

7 A bald eagle nest in Florida, U.S.A., weighed almost three tons (2.7 t)— about as much as 30 adult men.

8 Vultures pee on their legs to cool off when it's hot.

9 Barn owls swallow their prey whole.

10 Scientists think the great horned owl's long, hornlike tufts of feathers help camouflage the bird in trees.

Colorful Facts

About

Coral Reefs

1

Coral are **soft-bodied animals** related to jellyfish and anemones.

2

The box jellyfish has thousands of **stinging cells** on its tentacles, making it the **most venomous** marine animal.

3

Bargibant's **pygmy seahorse** **camouflages** itself so well in its coral home that it went undiscovered until 1969.

4

Hawaiian squirrelfish defend their hiding spots inside reefs by **grinding their teeth,** which sounds like a **chattering squirrel.**

5

Brain coral gets its name because its shape and **grooved surface** look like a human brain.

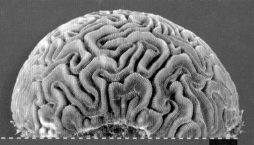

6

The piano fangblenny, a type of coral reef fish, **eats the mucus** of other fish.

7

Hawksbill turtles use their **pointed beaks** to **feast on sponges** that grow on coral reefs.

8

Coral gets its color from the **algae** that live **inside it.**

9

Coral use **tentacles** to **capture prey.**

Turn the page for more cool coral facts!

10
Scientists study coral fossils to learn about what the weather was like during prehistoric times.

11
Sponges that live on coral reefs produce chemicals that help fight human infections, including cancer.

12 Coral reefs make up just one percent of the ocean floor.

13 Coral reefs are home to about 25 percent of all marine life.

14 The **Great Barrier Reef** is as long as the **West Coast** of the United States.

15 British explorer **Captain James Cook** first saw the Great Barrier Reef after his **ship crashed** into it.

16 Coral **can live** up to **900 years.**

17 In Australia, a large **tower of coral** is called a **bommie.**

18 The **Bermuda Islands** are made from **ancient coral reefs** that formed 1.8 million years ago.

19 A marine animal called the **barrel sponge** is so large that a **human** could easily **fit inside one.**

20 The **mimic octopus** protects itself by changing its shape and color to **look like other animals.**

1

When the **RoboCup** competition was founded in 1997, the goal was to **have robots** advanced enough to **beat the best** human soccer players by 2050.

2

In the 1980s, **kids from** the island of **Koh Panyee, Thailand,** built a **floating soccer field** made out of wood.

3

About **250 million** people play soccer worldwide, making it the world's **most popular sport.**

4

The **first game with a ball** was played in Mesoamerica some 3,000 years ago— **the ball** was made from **tree resin.**

5

The **World Cup trophy** was first kept in a **bank vault** between World Cups, but it's now housed at the **FIFA World Football Museum** in Zurich, Switzerland.

6

A British man once set a world record by spending more than **48 hours** straight playing a soccer video game.

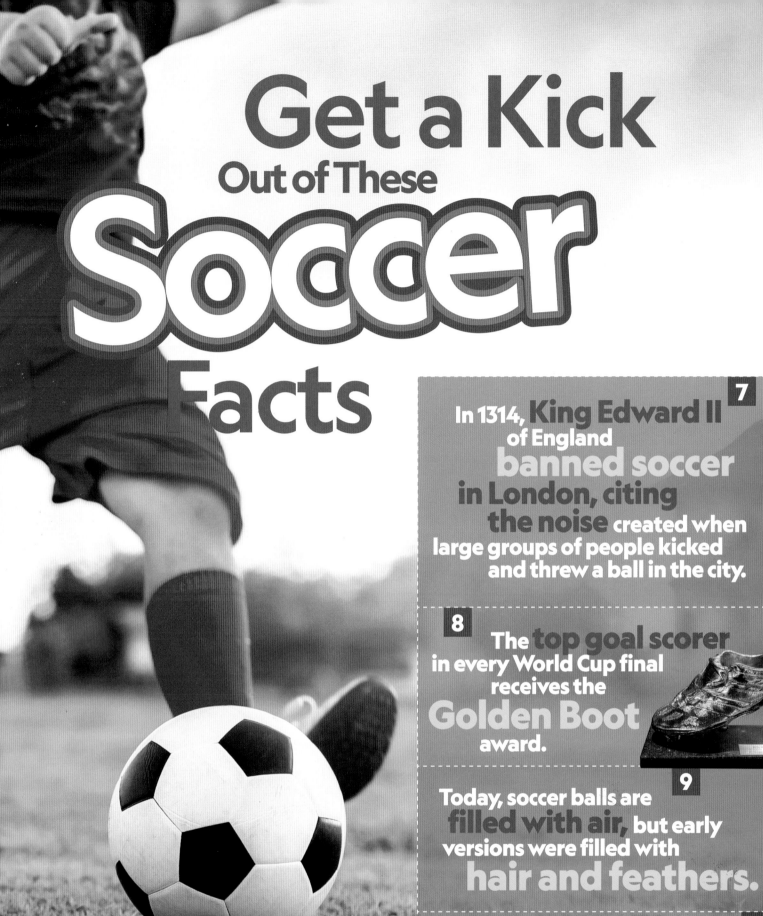

Get a Kick
Out of These
Soccer
Facts

7 In 1314, **King Edward II** of England **banned soccer** in London, citing **the noise** created when large groups of people kicked and threw a ball in the city.

8 The **top goal scorer** in every World Cup final receives the **Golden Boot** award.

9 Today, soccer balls are **filled with air,** but early versions were filled with **hair and feathers.**

10 It's said that in the early 1900s, a **soccer league** in the United States **paid its players 35 cents a goal.**

Naturally Pricey Facts

1 The rare **taaffeite** (pronounced tar-fite) gem— **only a handful** have ever been found—**sells for $2,500** for a single carat.

2 In 2014, a security guard protected the **world's largest white truffle** as it was flown from Italy to New York, U.S.A., where the more than **four-pound** (2-kg) **mushroom** sold for $61,000.

3 Some **meteorites** can fetch as much as **one million dollars per pound** (0.5 kg).

4 About two pounds (1 kg) of **vanilla beans** can cost **$400.**

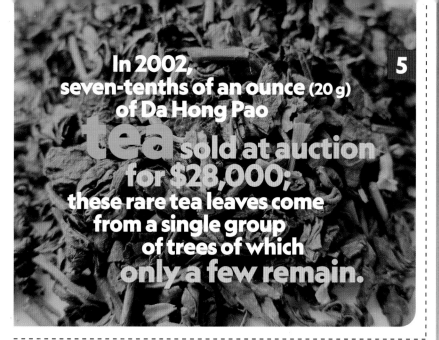

5

In 2002, seven-tenths of an ounce (20 g) of Da Hong Pao **tea** sold at auction for **$28,000;** these rare tea leaves come from a single group of trees of which **only a few remain.**

7

Used to **treat brain tumors** in humans, venom from the **deathstalker scorpion** sells for as much as **$39 million** per gallon because it is very difficult to harvest.

6

One pound (450 g) of the spice **saffron** can cost as much as **$5,000—** it's so expensive because **each tiny thread** of the spice is **hand-gathered** from saffron crocus flowers.

8

A three-foot (1-m)-long piece of what was thought to be **20-million-year-old fossilized poop** sold for **more than $10,000.** (It was later found to be fossilized plant matter.)

9

Hard-to-find **red diamonds** rarely sell for less than **$100,000.**

10

Abandoned **swiftlet nests,** which are made with the bird's saliva and **used in a delicacy** called **bird's nest soup,** can cost as much as $1,000 per 2.2 pounds (1 kg).

1 **The sun** has **enough energy** to burn for about **five billion more years.**

2 **Pluto** is **not very big—** only half as wide as the United States.

3 You could fit **one million Earths** inside the sun.

4 The **Milky Way galaxy** is orbiting a **giant black hole** that is surrounded by about **10,000 more** black holes.

5 **Jupiter** is more than **twice as big** as all the other **planets combined.**

6 **The winds** on **Neptune** travel faster than the **speed of sound.**

Surprising
Facts About the
Solar System

7
When an **asteroid is captured** by a planet's gravitational pull, it can **become a moon** of that planet.

8
Some **asteroids** are **hundreds of miles wide,** while others are as small as **pebbles.**

9
The **solar system** is about **4.5 billion years old**—young compared to the more than **13-billion-year-old** universe.

10
Sometimes **rocks from Mars** crash into Earth after asteroid strikes knock them off the red planet.

Say G'Day
to Awesome Facts
About
Australia

124

1 The **Australian Alps** have more area covered in snow than Switzerland's Alps.

2 The quokka, a marsupial found on Rottnest Island, Australia, has been labeled the "happiest animal in the world."

3 There are more than twice as many **kangaroos** as there are humans in Australia.

4 Australia is the only continent on Earth without an **active volcano.**

5 **Koalas,** which live in Australia's eucalyptus forests, get most of the water they need from eating leaves.

6 During a melon festival in Chinchilla, Australia, people ski down a hillside using **watermelons** as the skis.

7 Mount Disappointment in Wandong, Australia, was named for the disappointing **view** at its peak.

8 The northwestern tip of Tasmania, an island state of Australia, has the **cleanest air** in the world.

9 Bacteria and algae turn Western Australia's Lake Hillier **bubblegum pink** during the summer.

10 Australia is home to 21 of the 25 **most venomous snakes** in the world.

1

Apollo 13 astronauts used **duct tape** to **repair the air filtration** system on their spacecraft during their troubled 1970 mission— **a life-saving remedy.**

2

Police **use the fumes** from warmed **superglue** to make **fingerprints** visible.

3

Fish scales can be used to **make glue.**

4

Velcro became popular after **NASA used it** inside space helmets for **astronauts** to **scratch their noses.**

5

Resin, the sticky stuff that **oozes from trees,** is an ingredient in some **toothpastes.**

6

The **sea hare**— a species of **sticky slug**— can weigh **30 pounds** (14 kg).

7

Our lungs produce about **three ounces** (100 mL) **of mucus** per day— about as much as a **small juice box**— to trap germs.

Facts That Will Stick With You

8

Elmer's glue has a **cow on the bottle** because the glue was once **made from milk.**

9

A frog's **ultra-sticky tongue** can **snag insect prey faster** than a human **can blink.**

10

A substance based on the **slime that hagfish spew** to clog predators' gills might one day be used as a **protective coating** for divers.

What's the Difference?

FREEZING RAIN VS. SLEET VS. HAIL

Icy drops are falling. Is it freezing rain, or sleet, or hail? When rain falls through a thin layer of cold air, the drops don't have enough time to completely freeze. That's freezing rain. If the layer of air is thicker, the drops have enough time to freeze into sleet before hitting the ground. Hail, on the other hand, happens when a raindrop high in a cloud starts to freeze and then is pushed upward by strong winds, hitting more water droplets as it rises. As the process repeats itself, the pellet gets bigger and bigger until it is too heavy to stay aloft. Then, watch out! You can get walloped with hail the size of a small pea or a large softball.

Hail

BUTTER VS. MARGARINE

Butter and margarine are both pale yellow and can be spread on toast. They are essential ingredients for bakers and cooks everywhere. But while they may look and taste similar, their makeup is different. Butter is a dairy product, made by churning cream or milk. Shaking and turning the cream or milk causes the fats and liquids to separate, leaving thick, rich butter. Humans have been eating butter made from the milk of goats and sheep—and later cows—for 10,000 years. We use it to flavor our pancakes and to oil our pans before frying up eggs. Margarine didn't make its way into the kitchen until 1869, when a French chemist found a cheaper way to make a buttery product from beef fat mixed with vegetable oils. (Today's margarine leaves out the beef fat.) Margarine is naturally white, and to make it appear more "buttery," yellow coloring is added. During World War II, when butter was scarce, Americans began buying more margarine. Today, both are popular. There is debate over which one is healthier because each contains different types of fats. Cooks and bakers tend to split the difference, keeping both stocked in their kitchens.

CRICKET VS. BASEBALL

Grab a bat and a ball and get ready to play! But which sport—a rowdy game of cricket or a rousing game of baseball? Both are team sports, and in both games, players try to hit balls to score runs while the opposing team tries to get players out so they don't score. In cricket, bowlers throw balls to try to knock two small horizontal pieces called bails off the top of three sticks called wickets, and batters try to stop the bails from getting knocked down. In baseball, pitchers throw balls past batters who try to hit the balls and then run around four bases. Another difference—scores in baseball rarely go above 20, but in cricket they can be in the hundreds.

Cricket

BACTERIA VS. VIRUSES

Bacteria and viruses are both microbes—tiny living things that are so small you can't see them without a microscope. But other than being mini, these two kinds of microbes don't have much in common. Bacteria live almost everywhere on Earth, even in our bodies. There are about as many bacterial cells in your body as human cells. The fact that you are crawling with bacteria isn't bad, though. Most of them help keep you healthy. These good bacteria digest food, make vitamins, and keep out bad bacteria that make you sick. For example, bad bacteria can give you strep throat and ear infections. But medicines called antibiotics can kill these bacteria. Viruses also cause a lot of diseases. They cause mild ones, like the common cold, and serious ones, like COVID-19 and measles. Unfortunately, antibiotics don't work on viruses, but vaccines can prevent many illnesses that viruses cause. And washing your hands can help prevent the spread of both bad bacteria and viruses. Bring on the bubbles!

Yeti

SASQUATCH VS. YETI

It's time to play "Name That Cryptid." What's a cryptid? That's just a fancy term for legendary animals that people claim to have seen, but for which we don't have fossils, dead bodies, or live animals to prove they exist. Both sasquatch and yeti are terms for large, hairy creatures that make their homes in dense forests. The difference between them comes down to location. Sasquatch—also known as Bigfoot—is a creature said to be seen in the Pacific Northwest of North America. The yeti—also called the Abominable Snowman—is said to be spotted in the Himalaya in Asia. Some people say that sasquatch is more apelike, while the yeti is more like a bear.

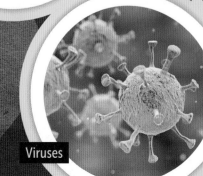
Viruses

JAGUAR VS. LEOPARD VS. CHEETAH

It's not always easy to tell the difference between a leopard, a jaguar, and a cheetah. However, a few basic facts can help single out these spotted big cats. Jaguars are usually dark yellow in color, but they can be brown or even black. Their fur has spots called rosettes because the pattern—a big spot surrounded by smaller spots—looks like a rose. Jaguars are stocky and more muscular than leopards or cheetahs, but they are the shortest of all the big cats. They live mostly in South America. Leopards look a lot like jaguars, but they are smaller (though not shorter). Their rosettes are smaller and form a closer cluster. Leopards live in Africa and Asia. Cheetahs have solid black spots on tan fur. They are the fastest land animal, built for speed with slender bodies and long legs. Cheetahs live in Africa and parts of Iran. Can you spot the differences now?

Cheetah

Jaguar

Leopard

The tiny globe skimmer dragonfly migrates **11,000 miles** (17,700 km) back and forth across the Indian Ocean— the longest migration of any insect— to follow the seasonal rainfall it needs in order to reproduce.

1

2 Bar-headed geese have **extra-large lungs** and more efficient breathing to help them migrate over the Himalaya, the world's highest mountain range.

3 The arctic tern has the longest recorded **round-trip migration,** a 44,000-mile (70,811-km) route that zigzags from Antarctica to Greenland.

4 Each year, the U.S. Forest Service closes two roads in the Shawnee National Forest in southern Illinois, so timber rattlesnakes, copperheads, and cottonmouth snakes can **migrate safely** to their summer feeding grounds.

PLEASE BRAKE FOR SNAKES

5 Each year, the bar-tailed godwit crosses the Pacific Ocean from Alaska, U.S.A., to New Zealand in a nine-day **nonstop flight,** without food or drink.

6 Migrating **monarch butterflies** roost in trees at night, and each year's new generation roosts in the same areas as the previous year's butterflies.

Moving Facts About Migration

7 **Zooplankton** float each night to the **ocean's surface** to feed, and then return to deep water in the morning to **hide from predators.**

8 As many as **10 million** straw-colored **fruit bats** darken the skies in Zambia's Kasanka National Park between October and December each year to **feast on fruit trees.**

9 Scientists think **birds take hundreds** of daily **"power naps,"** lasting only a few seconds each, to make up for lost sleep during long migrations.

10 No single monarch butterfly **lives long enough** to make an entire migration; it takes four or five generations to **complete the journey.**

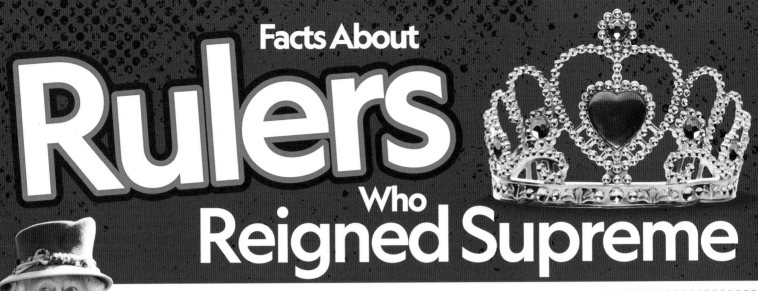

Facts About Rulers
Who Reigned Supreme

1 Britain's **Queen Elizabeth II** celebrates her birthday **twice:** once on her actual birthday in April, and again in June when the **weather is better.**

2 Fifteenth-century European ruler **Vlad III Dracula** is believed to be **the inspiration** for the famous **fictional vampire.**

3 In medieval England, Queen Elizabeth I served **gingerbread men** that looked like her **distinguished guests.**

4 The **Sultan of Brunei** owns the **world's largest** residential palace, with 1,788 rooms and 257 bathrooms.

5 In the 1970s, **Queen Margrethe II** of Denmark illustrated the Danish edition of *The Lord of the Rings.*

In the 13th century, **King Henry III** of England kept a **polar bear,** which **hunted for fish** in the River Thames.

6

7 Iolani Palace, the **only royal palace** in the United States, was home to the last ruling monarchs of what was until 1895 the **Kingdom of Hawaii.**

8 **King Tutankhamun** (or King Tut) has been nicknamed Egypt's Boy King because his **reign began** when he was **nine years old.**

9 In Britain, **all swans** without designated owners belong to **the queen.**

10 Albert II, **Prince of Monaco,** has **competed** in five **winter Olympics** in bobsledding.

1
Elephant calves sometimes **suck their trunk** for comfort, like human kids **suck their thumb.**

2
An **elephant's trunk** is strong enough to **push down a tree.**

3
Asian elephants sometimes **hold branches** in their trunks to **swat flies** away.

4
Some elephants—called big tuskers— grow **extra-long tusks** that **touch the ground.**

5
An elephant's **trunk** can hold two gallons (7.6 L) of water— as much as **32 glasses** of liquid.

6
African elephants' ears are **shaped like** the **African continent.**

7
An African elephant's **heart weighs** up to **46 pounds** (21 kg).

8
An elephant can use hundreds of **subtle signals** and movements—like curling its trunk or folding its ear— **while playing** with other elephants.

9
Elephant **tusks never stop** growing.

10
Elephants sometimes **greet each other** by **wrapping their trunks** together.

Exceptional
Facts About
Elephants

Gold Rush

Facts to Dig Into

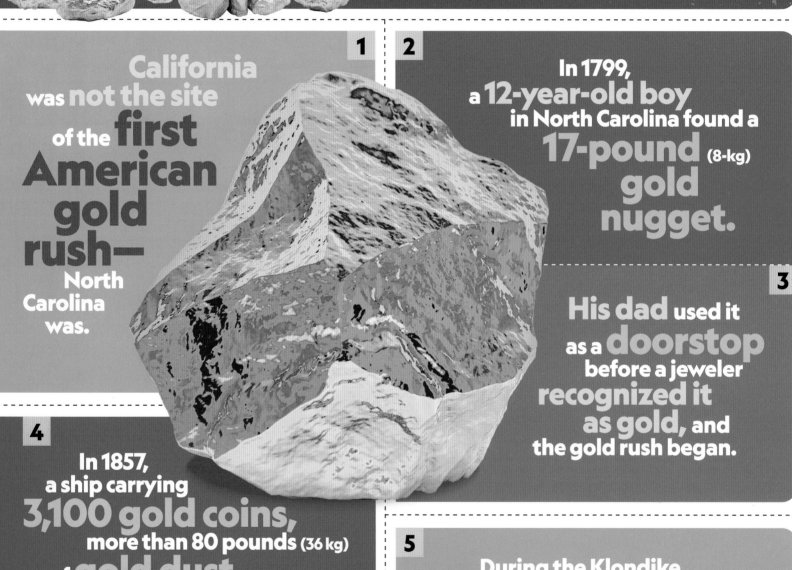

1 California was **not the site** of the **first American gold rush—** North Carolina was.

2 In 1799, a **12-year-old boy** in North Carolina found a **17-pound** (8-kg) **gold nugget.**

3 **His dad** used it as a **doorstop** before a jeweler recognized it **as gold,** and the gold rush began.

4 In 1857, a ship carrying **3,100 gold coins,** more than 80 pounds (36 kg) of **gold dust,** and 45 **gold bars** from the California gold rush sank off the coast of South Carolina— the recovered treasure is worth more than **$50 million today.**

5 During the Klondike gold rush in Canada, a **scam artist** set up **fake telegraph** poles and wires and took prospectors' money to **"wire" messages home.**

136

Blue jeans **6** were invented as **sturdy work pants** for gold rush **miners** in California.

7 At the height of **California's gold rush,** as gold diggers came to the state and **farmers had trouble** meeting food demands, a single chicken **egg could cost $1—** the equivalent of about **$30** today.

8 The San Francisco 49ers, named for the **1849** **gold rush,** have won **five** **Super Bowls.**

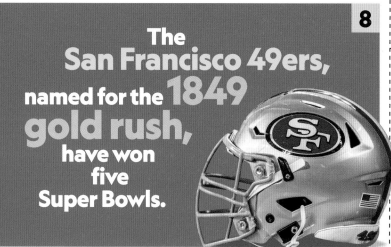

10

Rabbit Creek in Yukon, Canada, was renamed **Bonanza Creek** after **gold** was found there in 1896.

9

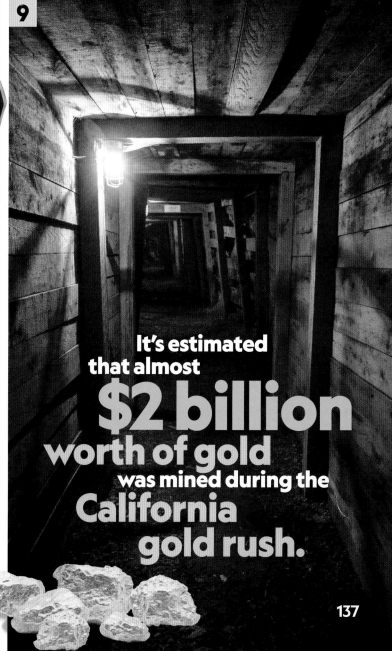

It's estimated that almost **$2 billion** worth of gold was mined during the **California gold rush.**

1

A tree-dwelling ant from Southeast Asia **explodes** when attacked, **spewing its enemies** with sticky, toxic goo.

2

When threatened, some sea cucumbers **poop out their guts,** which entangle predators. (The organs quickly regenerate.)

3

The potato beetle **eats a plant** that is poisonous to its predators and then coats itself in its **poisonous poop.**

4

Wolverine frogs **break their own bones** and then poke them through their skin to **use as claws.**

5

When some **wasps are threatened,** they give off a **chemical alarm** that calls other wasps to come help sting the attacker.

6

With just **one kick** of its foot, the cassowary, an Australian bird, **can slice open a predator** using a **four-inch-long** (10-cm) **claw.**

7

The shock of an **electric eel** could **knock a horse** off its feet.

8

One type of lizard **shoots blood from its eyes** when threatened to confuse predators and to give the lizard a chance to escape.

9

Porcupines charge backward into predators because their sharp **quills point backward.**

10
Tarantulas
sometimes spin "trip wires" over their burrows to alert them to prey passing overhead.

Sharp and Stinging
Facts About Animal
Defenses

1 Some scientists believe that ancient **Egyptian astronomers** used stars' positions in the sky to **align the Pyramids** at Giza to true north.

2 The Great Pyramid of Giza is **the only** one of the **Seven Wonders** of the Ancient World **still standing.**

3 The **2,000-year-old** Great Pyramid of Cholula, located in what is now Mexico, is as wide as **nine Olympic swimming pools** but lies hidden under trees, grass, and soil.

4 **Sudan has more** pyramids **than Egypt.**

5 The **Pyramid of the Sun,** built by ancient Mesoamericans, has a **network of tunnels** under it that lead to a chamber that may have been used for funeral rituals.

6 Some Egyptians who built the pyramids **were paid** in **radishes, onions,** and **garlic.**

7 When a 16th-century **Spanish explorer** saw the Chavín temple, an ancient flat-topped pyramid in Peru, he thought it was created **by giants.**

Ancient
Facts About
Pyramids

Chichen Itza

8

Sudan pyramids have **elephants and giraffes** etched on their bases, which shows that the desert was once a **lush grassland.**

9

The **Maya and Aztec** built pyramids on top of their **older pyramids.**

10

If you **clap your hands** at the base of the Chichen Itza pyramid, it sounds like a flock of **chirping birds.**

1

Modeled after **termite mounds,** an office building in Zimbabwe has holes that allow the structure to draw in cool air and expel hot air.

2

Fish fins, which are as sensitive as human fingertips, could help scientists improve the ability of **underwater robots** to explore the oceans.

3

Scientists are developing a **painless needle** for shots based on a mosquito's stinger.

4

Scientists are designing underwater sensors, based on the frequencies **dolphins** use to communicate, to transmit tsunami warnings from deep in the ocean back to land.

5

Scientists are learning how to make strong, nontoxic glue based on the **sticky substance** mussels use to attach themselves to rocks and boat bottoms.

Mind-Blowing
Facts About
Biomimicry

8 Scientists at Stanford University, in California, U.S.A., climbed walls using hand and foot attachments based on **gecko feet,** which contain an adhesive that grips tight but releases easily for the next step.

7 A tiny beetle in the Namib desert that **collects moisture** in grooves on its back and channels the moisture to its mouth is a model for engineers on how to harvest **water from the air.**

10 A company in Colombia made a firm but flexible backpack based on the overlapping shells **on an armadillo's back.**

6 A new type of **window glass** is clear to humans but looks like a **spiderweb to birds,** which keeps them from flying into the glass and getting hurt.

9 The flexible wings of the **rose butterfly,** which must absorb sunlight to fly, inspired a super-efficient design for **solar cells.**

Blue Volcano

When a volcano on the tiny Indonesian island of **Krakatau erupted** in August 1883, it could be heard **thousands of miles away.**

More than 10 million people live in Jakarta—Indonesia's city with the **largest population.** That's about **two million more** people than are living in New York City.

A strange eruption creates a dazzling light show.

The night is pitch-black. But the dark slopes of a hill inside the crater of Kawah Ijen volcano in Indonesia, a country in Asia, are lit up like a holiday light show. Tourists flock to the volcano to see what look like glowing blue rivers of lava. But they aren't rivers of lava. They're rivers of glowing sulfur.

BURNING BLUE

Glowing red lava flowing from an erupting volcano isn't unusual. Glowing sulfur is. Hot, sulfur-rich gases escape constantly from cracks called fumaroles in Kawah Ijen's crater. The gases cool when they hit the air. Some condense into liquid sulfur, which flows down the hillside. When the sulfur and leftover gases ignite, they burn bright blue and light up the night sky. Scientists were told that sulfur miners on the volcano sometimes use torches to ignite the sulfur. The blue flames make Kawah Ijen popular with tourists, who watch from a safe distance. Recently scientists confirmed that some of the sulfur and gases also burn naturally, igniting as hot gases combine with oxygen in the air.

VOLCANO MINERS

Sulfur is a common volcanic gas, and its chemical properties are used to manufacture many things, such as rubber. But it's so plentiful in Kawah Ijen's crater that miners make a dangerous daily trek into the crater to collect sulfur from a fumarole near an acid lake. They use ceramic pipes to move the gases from the fumarole. Then they spray the pipes with water from a spring. This cools the gases and causes them to condense into molten sulfur. The sulfur then cools and hardens into rock. Using this method, miners get more usable rock faster than if they just collected scattered pieces. They smash up the rock with metal bars, stuff the pieces into baskets, and carry them out of the crater on their backs. The loads are heavy—between 100 and 200 pounds (45 to 91 kg) apiece.

READING THE DANGER ZONE

Miners face another danger: a huge eruption. Kawah Ijen's last big eruption was more than 200 years ago, but the volcano is still active. A big eruption could endanger hundreds of miners and tourists. Indonesian scientists want to find a way to predict a big eruption in time to keep everyone safe. But the deep acid lake makes it difficult to pick up the usual signals that warn of a coming volcanic eruption. For example, certain gases are usually more abundant right before an eruption. But in this lake, those gases dissolve in the deep water before they can register on the geologist's monitoring equipment. As scientists search for ways to predict this unusual volcano's behavior, Kawah Ijen's blue fires continue to attract audiences who appreciate the volcano's amazing glow.

HOW KAWAH IJEN ERUPTS

Earth's outer shell is broken into a jigsaw puzzle of several tectonic plates, or gigantic slabs of rock, that move constantly. In Indonesia, the oceanic Australian plate slips under the Eurasian plate at a subduction zone. As the Australian plate slides deep down, heat generated in Earth's interior makes the plate superhot, and parts of it melt. This melted rock, called magma, rises toward Earth's surface. Pressure on the magma lessens as it rises, allowing gases inside to expand, which can lead to explosive volcanic eruptions.

More than 70 active volcanoes are in Indonesia.

Indonesia is a group of more than 17,500 islands off the coast of Southeast Asia. It is the largest country in the region.

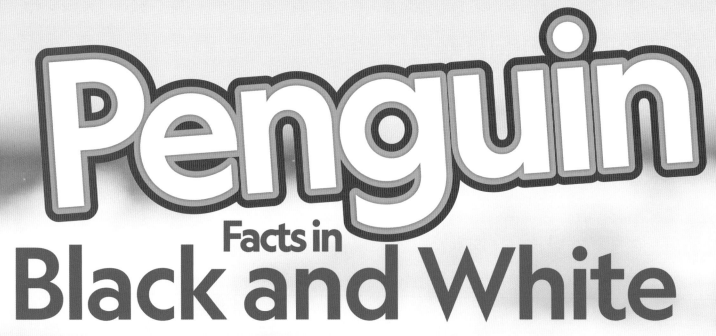

Penguin

Facts in
Black and White

1 Little blue penguins, also called **fairy penguins,** are the world's **smallest penguins** at only about 13 inches (33 cm) tall.

2 Adélie penguin **poop,** **colored pink** from the krill they eat, is so bright scientists can **see it from space.**

3 A **colony of penguins** is called a **waddle** when it's on land and a **raft** when it's in the water.

4 A now extinct **giant penguin** was as big as an adult **human.**

5

One colony of **chinstrap penguins,** located in the Sandwich Islands, contains more than **a million breeding pairs.**

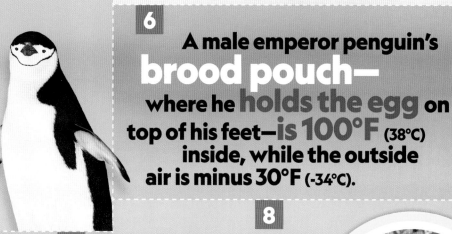

6

A male emperor penguin's **brood pouch—** where he **holds the egg** on top of his feet—**is 100°F** (38°C) inside, while the outside air is minus 30°F (-34°C).

7

Galápagos penguins **hold their flippers over their toes** to keep their webbed feet from getting **burned** by the hot sun.

8

New Zealand's Fiordland crested penguins, or tawakis, nest under rocks and fallen trees— they are the **only penguins** that **live in rainforests.**

9

An **emperor penguin once dove** to **1,850 feet** (564 m)—most emperor penguin dives are only to about 650 feet (198 m).

10

There are **no penguins** at the North Pole.

Terrific Facts About
Turning Trash Into Treasure

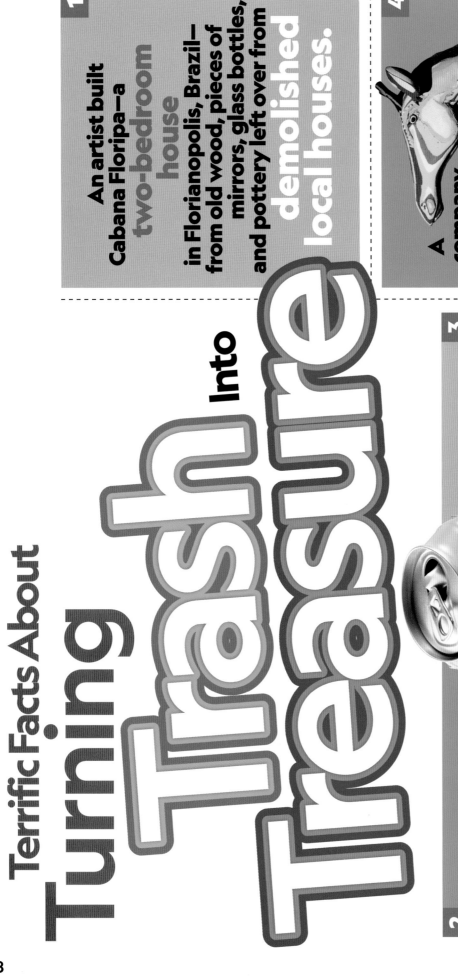

1 An artist built Cabana Floripa—a **two-bedroom house** in Florianopolis, Brazil—from old wood, pieces of mirrors, glass bottles, and pottery left over from **demolished local houses.**

4 A company in Nairobi, Kenya, takes **old flip-flops** and uses them to create artwork such as **4.5-foot-tall (1.4-m) giraffes.**

3 **Mount Trashmore** in Cedar Rapids, Iowa, U.S.A., offers trails and a **scenic overlook** on a **mountain made of compacted trash.**

2 Upcycle **food scraps** made into **tasty dishes,** like a pizza company in Brooklyn, New York, U.S.A., that uses **bruised vegetables** to make sauces.

5

Plastic bottles can be turned into yarn

used to make puffy jackets, pants, and shoes.

6

Craftspeople turn old plastic bags into reusable tote bags, mats to sleep on, and decorative baskets.

7

Old coffee or tea cups can become bird feeders or birdbaths.

8

Colorful paper from old magazines can be rolled up to create decorative bowls.

9

Visitors to Magic Gardens in Philadelphia, Pennsylvania, U.S.A., walk along paths with walls embedded with bicycle parts, glass bottles, mirrors, and other reused trash.

10

A designer in London uses surplus **army parachutes** to create fashionable clothes.

Perplexing
Facts About
Puzzles
and
Codes

1 Code breakers at Bletchley Park in Britain solved the Germans' **Enigma code,** which experts think **shortened World War II** by at least **two years.**

2 Tony Fisher, a British puzzlemaker, built a **five-foot** (1.5-m)-**tall Rubik's Cube** using the same materials as in the handheld version.

7 There are **255,168 ways** to fill out a **tic-tac-toe** game board.

3 President Thomas Jefferson **developed a code** using the keyword **"artichokes"** so that Meriwether Lewis could **send secret messages** during the 1804–1806 expedition to map part of the American Northwest—but there is no evidence it was ever used.

8 The Culper **spy network** operated during the **American Revolution** to pass information about the British to General George Washington—the spies wrote in **invisible ink** and used a **number system** to identify one another.

4 Roman leader **Julius Caesar** shifted letters by a set number to create a coded message that took some **800 years** to crack.

9 In 1762, the **first jigsaw puzzle** was made by mounting a **map of England** on a piece of wood and cutting out the counties for kids to reassemble.

5 **"Fun"** was the number one "across" answer in the world's **first crossword puzzle,** which was created by a *New York World* journalist in 1913.

10 Written in the 1400s, the Voynich manuscript uses **an alphabet nobody** has been able to **understand.**

6 The **"Kryptos" sculpture,** located at the Central Intelligence Agency's headquarters outside Washington, D.C., contains an **encrypted message**—and one small part remains undeciphered.

Catchy Facts About
Famous
Musicians

In 2005,
Paul McCartney became

the first musician to broadcast a concert into space when it was transmitted to the International Space Station.

1

3

Taylor Swift grew up on a **Christmas tree farm.**

2

Prince liked the color purple because it represented royalty, and had a song and album with "purple" in the title.

4

Queen singer **Freddie Mercury** dedicated his solo album to his cats.

Before she sings, **5** **Selena Gomez** sometimes takes **a sip of olive oil**— she says it helps her voice.

6 **Dolly Parton** once **lost** in a Dolly Parton **look-alike** contest.

7 The cries of **Jay-Z's newborn daughter Blue Ivy** appear on his song "Glory."

8 A lock of **Elvis's hair** sold for **$115,000** in 2002.

9 **Elton John** has a **walk-in closet** to store his **sunglasses.**

10 **Six years before** *Hamilton* opened on Broadway, **Lin-Manuel Miranda** rapped an **early version** of one of its songs for President Barack Obama **at the White House.**

1 China gifted Washington, D.C.'s Smithsonian National Zoo two **giant pandas** after U.S. president **Richard Nixon** visited the country in 1972.

2 At the San Diego Zoo in California, U.S.A., giraffes eat **real acacia leaves** hung high in **fake trees.**

3 On hot days at some zoos, big cats are given **"bloodsicles,"** or blocks of **frozen blood,** to chew on.

4 Omaha's Henry Doorly Zoo in Nebraska, U.S.A., is home to the world's largest **indoor swamp—** and nine American alligators— under a **13-story dome.**

5 An Asian **elephant** named Lucky celebrated her **60th birthday** with a **large cake** made of fruits and vegetables at the San Antonio Zoo in Texas, U.S.A.

6 **Koko,** a western lowland gorilla born at the San Francisco Zoo in California in 1971, learned how to **communicate** with sign language.

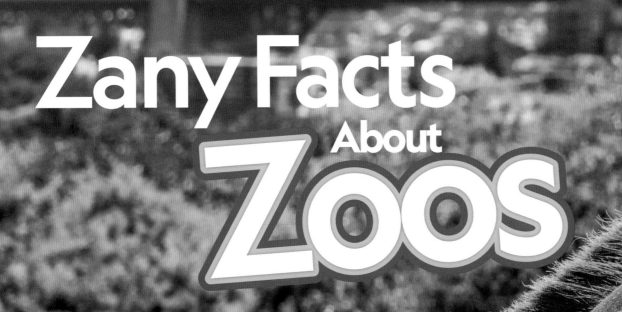

Zany Facts
About
Zoos

7 **Giraffes** at Taronga Zoo in Sydney, Australia, were given wreaths covered in **foliage** and **apples** as a **Christmas treat.**

8 A school of **poop-eating** tilapia fish help keep the 70,000-gallon (265,000-L) **hippo pool** clean at the Cincinnati Zoo in Ohio, U.S.A.

9 **Flamingos** at Zoo Miami in Florida, U.S.A., were **sheltered** from a **hurricane** in a restroom.

10 New York City's Bronx Zoo set a world record in 2016 with its display of **78,564 origami elephants.**

155

Dig These Facts About Fossils

1

A **fossilized bone** doesn't contain any bone—over many years, the bone has **turned to rock.**

2

One huge coprolite— **fossilized poop—** was **17 inches** (43 cm) **long** and 6 inches (15 cm) **wide** and thought to be a dropping from a *Tyrannosaurus rex.*

3

Paleontologists call **fragments** of dinosaur bones **too broken up to identify** "chunkasaurus."

4

Some mythological creatures, such as **centaurs, griffins, and cyclops,** may have been **inspired by fossils.**

5

Scientists can tell **how much an animal weighed** by studying its fossilized **footprints.**

6

The American Museum of Natural History in New York City stores fossils in a **10-story building—** seven of those stories contain **only dinosaur bones.**

7

Paleontologists discovered the fossil of a **three-foot-tall (1-m) parrot** and named it **Squawkzilla.**

8

While walking on a beach in England in 2009, **five-year-old** Daisy Morris found a fossil of an **unknown pterosaur—** scientists named it *Vectidraco daisymorrisae* after her.

9

Scientists found 3.5-billion-year-old **fossilized bacteria** in Australia that may be the **oldest known life** on Earth.

10

Dinosaur fossils have been found on **every continent,** and about **50 new species** are discovered **each year.**

Extreme Weirdness

VADER RULES THE SKY

WHAT Hot-air balloon festival

WHERE León, Mexico

DETAILS This might be the Rebels' worst nightmare. Participants at this festival soared across the sky in giant hot-air balloons, such as this one shaped like Darth Vader's mask. More than a hundred balloons fly each year—anything from pandas to bees to scarecrows. But don't worry. This Vader's only full of hot air.

WOMAN WALKS ON AIR

WHAT Art illusion

WHERE Lodz, Poland

DETAILS Look out below! Artist Regina Silveira of Brazil specializes in creating optical illusions. Her piece, titled "Depth," makes it look as if she's floating inside a tall building. A digitally generated image on the flat floor makes it seem as if the room extends several stories below her feet. That's some smart art.

COZY CLUCKERS

WHAT Sweaters for hens

WHERE Norwich, England

DETAILS Word on the farm is that wool sweaters for chickens are all the rage. People across England knitted "woolly jumpers" for rescued hens that had lost feathers from stressful living conditions. About 1,500 hens were fitted with sweaters of all designs—stripes, bows, and even a few holiday themes.

BLOOMS ON WHEELS

WHAT Flower parade

WHERE Zundert, Netherlands

DETAILS What's that smell? Flowers—lots of them. Every year some 50,000 people head to this Dutch town to see an elaborate parade of petals. In addition to giraffes and other animals, the floats are shaped like giant monsters, cityscapes, motorcycles, ships, and yes, even flowers. Best-smelling parade ever.

BIGGEST HAT EVER

WHAT Ice-cream carton headgear

WHERE Ascot, England

DETAILS Some people eat out of ice-cream cartons—this woman wears them. Huge hats are popular at Royal Ascot, an English horse racing event. Among the hats worn by the crowd was this gigantic one, made of gold spray-painted ice-cream cartons. Wonder what she did with all that ice cream?

TREE STOPS TRAFFIC

WHAT Traffic light tree

WHERE London, England

DETAILS Money doesn't grow on trees—but traffic lights might! This 26-foot (8-m)-high treelike structure is made of 75 sets of traffic lights controlled by computers. The sculpture, created by a French artist to represent the energy of the city around it, has been a big hit with locals. Sounds like this fake tree has really taken root.

Facts About Famous Firsts

The first

McDonald's hamburger,
made in 1948, cost 15 cents.

1

2

The **first airplane,** the Wright Flyer, was in the air

for only **12 seconds** on its first flight.

3

In 1895, **Annie Londonderry—** who had never ridden a bicycle before— became the **first woman** to **ride around the world** on one.

4

The first **box of crayons,** sold in 1903, had **only eight colors:** black, brown, blue, red, purple, orange, yellow, and green.

5 The first **text message** was **"Merry Christmas."**

6 Astronaut **Buzz Aldrin** took the first **space selfie** in 1966 while on the Gemini 12 mission.

7 When **electric lights** were first installed in the **White House,** in 1891, President Benjamin Harrison and his wife, Caroline, refused to touch the switches for fear of **getting shocked.**

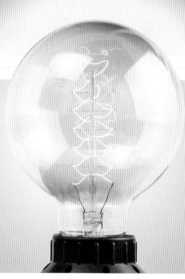

8 When scientist Robert Plot discovered the first **dinosaur bone** in 1677, he thought it was the bone of a **giant human.**

9 The **first cell phone weighed 2.5 pounds** (1.1 kg), about **six times the weight** of today's smartphones.

10 Victoria Woodhull ran for United States **president** almost **50 years before a** constitutional amendment gave women **the right to vote.**

1 Maglev trains use **magnetic fields** to **levitate trains** above the tracks, allowing them to travel at high speeds.

2 In Japan, professional **"subway pushers"** pack passengers into **crowded trains.**

3 New York City buses **don't accept paper money** because the giant vacuum hoses used to empty the fare boxes would **shred the bills.**

4 The **largest bus** in the world is 72 feet (22 m) long, can **carry 300 passengers,** and has three segments so it can bend on tight turns.

5 Parts of some **train wheels** were once **made of paper.**

Rev Your Engine
With These Facts About
Vehicles

6 Engineers in Slovakia built a **car** that can **transform into** an **airplane.**

7 After a man **wrecked his car** in the desert in Morocco in 1993, he built a **functioning motorcycle** out of the **car parts** and rode it to safety.

8 The first **cars did not have steering wheels;** they were guided by joystick-like levers.

9 In Britain, **ghost trains** sometimes run **without passengers.**

10 Some airplanes have **hidden bedrooms** where the **flight crew sleeps** during long flights.

What's the Difference?

Check out these similar pairings and see how you can determine this from that!

EMU VS. OSTRICH

While these big birds may look alike, they're worlds apart. Emus are found mostly in Australia, but also in New Guinea, Indonesia, the Solomon Islands, and the Philippines. Ostriches live in African savannas and deserts. Though emus and ostriches may never cross paths, they do have plenty in common. For example, neither bird can fly, but both are quick on their feet. Emus can run up to 30 miles an hour (48 km/h). Ostriches can run up to 43 miles an hour (69 km/h), and they use their wings as "rudders" to steer and change direction while running. Both ostriches and emus have powerful legs. An ostrich kick is strong enough to kill a lion. And emus are the only bird with calf muscles! But these birds of a feather have one big difference—their size. An emu tips the scales at 100 pounds (45 kg), but that's nothing compared to the ostrich, which weighs up to 350 pounds (159 kg). It's the biggest bird on the planet.

Emu

IGNEOUS VS. SEDIMENTARY VS. METAMORPHIC ROCK

All rocks are not created equal. Rocks are classified into three groups: igneous, sedimentary, and metamorphic. Igneous rocks form when magma, or molten rock, slowly cools underground or when lava—magma that erupts from a volcano—cools on Earth's surface. Sedimentary rocks form when small bits of sand, rock, and mud accumulate in layers that fuse together over time. Metamorphic rocks have been changed from the extreme pressures deep in Earth's depths or by the motion of tectonic plates on the surface. Rocks can change form. For example, wind and water can erode igneous rocks into smaller pieces that are then deposited into layers that slowly turn into sedimentary rocks. If these rocks are pushed deep below Earth's surface, they become metamorphic rocks. Cool!

Metamorphic rock

WASP VS. HORNET VS. BEE

Wasps, hornets, and bees are all insects. But they have important differences, too. Wasps have a pointy end and a narrow "waist" that separates the two parts of their bodies. Some wasps are solitary, while others are social. Solitary wasps use their stinger to hunt other insects. Social wasps use their stinger only for defense. Hornets are a type of wasp, but they are usually a little bigger and fatter than most other wasps. All hornets are social. They chew wood into papery pulp and then use that pulp to build hives. They eat flies, bees, and other insects. Like other social wasps, hornets use their stinger only for defense. A single wasp or hornet can sting many times. Bees are rounder and plumper than wasps and have hairy bodies and legs. They collect pollen from plants. Like social wasps, bees use their stinger just for defense, but they can only use it once: They die after delivering a sting.

Bee

CLEMENTINES VS. TANGERINES VS. SATSUMA MANDARINS

Tangerines, clementines, and Satsuma mandarins all are members of the mandarin orange family. Clementines are the smallest and are seedless. They're known for their smooth, glossy peel and deep red-orange color. They sometimes go by the nicknames "cuties" and "sweeties" in the grocery store. Tangerines have a rougher, thinner skin, making them a little harder to peel. They're bright orange and more tart than clementines, with a few seeds. Satsuma mandarins, which were first grown in Japan 700 years ago, are a lighter orange. They're sweet and generally seedless. Their claim to fame is that they are the easiest variety to peel, but they're also more fragile and can damage easily if squished. Another thing all three share? They are chock-full of vitamin C!

Tangerine

ANTHROPOLOGY VS. ARCHAEOLOGY

What kind of scientist is likely to get really dirty on the job—an anthropologist or an archaeologist? Both academic disciplines study human beings. Anthropology is the study of human cultures—past and present. It includes the study of human biology, as well as how modern humans fit in among all the species on the human family tree. Anthropology also includes linguistics, the study of language. Archaeology is a branch of anthropology. It's the study of past cultures, which includes excavating ancient places such as the Pyramids of Giza in Egypt to learn about what these people believed and how they spent their days.

STALACTITE VS. STALAGMITE

It's no wonder people confuse stalactites and stalagmites—they're only separated by two letters! While these two cave features are similar in their outward appearance, they are formed differently. Luckily, there's a handy way to remember how to tell them apart. A stalactite hangs from the ceiling or sides of a cave like a giant icicle. It is commonly cone-shaped with a pointed tip and forms when water containing minerals from the cave's limestone rock walls slowly drips down. A stalagmite is the opposite of a stalactite. It looks like a spear with a rounded or flattened tip rising from the cave's floor. A stalagmite forms slowly over time as drips from a stalactite hit the floor. Sometimes a stalactite and stalagmite will connect and form a column. Still confused over which is which? Try this alphabet trick: Stalactite is spelled with a *c,* as in "ceiling"—it hangs from the ceiling. Stalagmite has the letter *g,* as in "ground"—it extends up from the ground.

Stalactites

Stalagmites

Odd Facts

About

Hoofed

Animals

1 Camels have two rows of extra-long eyelashes to keep out the desert sand.

2 The hippo's closest living relative is the whale.

3 Mother pigs sing to their babies.

4 A tapir uses its snout as a snorkel when swimming underwater.

5 Horses can't vomit.

6 A group of giraffes is called a tower.

7 When a goat is "kidding," it is giving birth— not telling a joke.

8 American bison, which can weigh up to 2,000 pounds (907 kg), are very agile and can jump high fences.

9 Some people believed that okapis were unicorns until scientists in the early 1900s identified the wary rainforest animal as the giraffe's only living relative.

10 The pattern of a zebra's coat confuses flies, making it hard for them to land.

1 **Running the bases** of a baseball diamond is a longer distance than running the length of a **football field.**

4 **Every new** major league **baseball** is **rubbed with mud** from a secret location along the Delaware River before it is used.

2 Major league **umpires** are required to **wear black underwear** in case their pants tear.

5 The first **baseball caps** were **made from straw.**

3 At the **swimming pool suite** at the Arizona Diamondbacks' stadium, paying guests can **go for a dip** while watching the game.

Baseball

Facts That Hit It
Out of the Park

6 A regulation **baseball** has **108 stitches.**

7 The average major league **baseball** is used for only **seven pitches.**

8 Instead of playing nine innings as we do today, baseball teams in the **early 19th century** played until **one team scored 21 runs.**

9 About **19 million hot dogs** are sold at major league baseball games every year.

10 In 1976, the **Chicago White Sox wore shorts** for three of their games, but switched back to pants after **players complained** of scraping their legs when **sliding into base.**

Engaging

Facts About

Europe

1

Bulgarians **shake their heads for "yes"** and nod their heads for "no."

2

Eighty-four percent of the British population **drinks tea** every day.

3

A **tooth, thumb,** and **finger** of astronomer **Galileo Galilei** are on display at the Galileo Museum in Florence, Italy.

4

In Spain, when **a child loses a tooth,** a mouse named **El Ratoncito Pérez** comes and leaves a gift under their pillow.

5

A bridge in Istanbul, Turkey, **connects** the continents of **Asia** and **Europe.**

6

There are **five times** more **bicycles than cars** in Copenhagen, Denmark.

7 In **cold weather,** the **Eiffel Tower** in Paris, France, **shrinks** approximately **six inches** (15 cm), but expands again when it gets warm.

8 More **chocolate** is sold in Belgium's **Brussels Airport** than anywhere else in the world.

9 There are **no mosquitoes** in Iceland.

10 Norway has **knighted three penguins,** all named Nils Olav.

museé du quai Branly

Gray seals use their flippers to propel themselves through the water, but their bodies move in a caterpillar-like motion

on land.

Cinematic

Facts About the
Silver Screen

1 In 1975, the movie **Jaws** became the first film to earn more than **$100 million** at the U.S. box office.

2 The first **"moving pictures"** were a **series of photographs** that showed horses galloping and birds flying.

3 At **K9 Cinemas** in Plano, Texas, U.S.A., you can **bring your dog** to the movies.

4 President Dwight D. Eisenhower watched more than **200 Westerns** in the **White House** movie theater during his presidency.

5 The **earliest movies were silent,** and when sound was added the movies became known as **"talkies."**

7

IMAX cameras have been into **space**, to the deepest part of the **ocean** and to the top of **Mount Everest**.

8

The **helicopter** landing pad on *Tis*, a designer yacht, can be transformed into an **outdoor movie theater**.

9

People watch movies on a grassy lawn surrounded by **graves** at the Hollywood **Forever Cemetery** in Los Angeles, California, U.S.A.

6

Before movies had sound, **popcorn wasn't allowed** to be eaten in theaters.

Admit One

Admit One

10

Sun Pictures in Broome, Australia, is the world's **oldest open-air movie theater,** showing movies outside since 1916.

Precious

Facts About

Presidential Pets

1 John F. Kennedy's dog Pushinka was the pup of one of the first dogs sent **into space.**

2 William McKinley had a **parrot** that could whistle **"Yankee Doodle."**

3 Warren G. Harding hosted a **birthday party** for his dog Laddie Boy at the White House.

4 Calvin Coolidge's pet raccoon wore a collar with the name **"White House Raccoon"** embroidered on it.

5 During World War I, Woodrow Wilson kept a **flock of sheep** on the White House lawn.

6

Lyndon B. Johnson's **beagles** were named **Him and Her.**

7

When Theodore Roosevelt's son Archie was sick, **his pony** was brought up to **his bedroom** in the White House for a visit.

8

Abraham Lincoln let his two **pet goats,** Nanny and Nanko, ride in the **presidential carriage.**

9

Herbert Hoover's family adopted a wild **opossum** that strayed onto the White House grounds **and named it Billy.**

10

William Taft's **pet cow,** which provided milk for the first family, was named **Pauline Wayne** and lived on the White House grounds.

1 A **sea urchin's** spines **help it move** along the seafloor.

2 The thistle's flower grows **spiny leaves** to protect itself from being **eaten by wildlife.**

3 A **jackfruit,** which is a yellow-green fruit with spiky skin, can weigh up to **100 pounds** (45 kg).

4 **Prickly pear cactus** is sometimes **used as a fence** to keep livestock from escaping.

5 The Spanish ribbed newt pokes its **sharp ribs through its skin** to **defend itself.**

6 A **crown-of-thorns starfish** can **regrow** up to half of its body if damaged.

7 **When threatened,** a potto bends its head to reveal **sharp vertebrae—** the primate can remain in this position for hours.

8 A porcupine's **quills are soft** when it's born, **but they harden** within a few days.

9 The **armadillo lizard** **rolls into a ball** when threatened, protecting itself with spines on its head and tail.

Prickly

Facts That Stick Out

10 Most species of **pufferfish,** which contain enough toxin to kill 30 humans, are **covered with small spines** that stick out when the animals **inflate.**

Scientists think that young humpback whales "whisper" to their mothers so that the pair

doesn't
attract the
attention
of nearby orcas,
or killer whales.

Behind the Facts

We're sure you're wondering how we got so many awesome facts about so many awesome topics into this book. First, we came up with a list of all the coolest and most interesting things out there—things we know kids want to know more about. Like captivating critters. Pirates. Toys, holidays, and bugs. Crazy hotels. Black holes. Cookies. The future. All kinds of stuff. Then we found 10 or 20 of the most exciting and surprising facts about those topics to arrange on each page. We carefully researched each and every fact to make sure it's absolutely true, and then we packed the book full of cool bonus content! Things like strange places, moments of extreme weirdness around the world, and a feature called "What's the Difference?" that will answer age-old questions like "What's the difference between a porcupine and a hedgehog?"

And we designed the pages so colorfully that you'll pore over them endlessly and will love flipping to all your favorite parts. And one last fact: It took a big team of writers, editors, photo researchers, and designers to make this book—the greatest book team around!

Illustration Credits

Index

Boldface indicates illustrations.

For Diane, the most fantastic mom —JB

For BHG, JRG, and GEG —MRH

For Zoomer, the world's weirdest cat —AH

Since 1888, the National Geographic Society has funded more than 14,000 research, conservation, education, and storytelling projects around the world. National Geographic Partners distributes a portion of the funds it receives from your purchase to National Geographic Society to support programs including the conservation of animals and their habitats. To learn more, visit natgeo.com/info.

For more information, visit nationalgeographic.com, call 1-877-873-6846, or write to the following address:

National Geographic Partners, LLC
1145 17th Street NW
Washington, DC 20036-4688 U.S.A.

For librarians and teachers: nationalgeographic.com/books/librarians-and-educators

More for kids from National Geographic: natgeokids.com

National Geographic Kids magazine inspires children to explore their world with fun yet educational articles on animals, science, nature, and more. Using fresh storytelling and amazing photography, *Nat Geo Kids* shows kids ages 6 to 14 the fascinating truth about the world—and why they should care. **natgeo.com/subscribe**

For rights or permissions inquiries, please contact National Geographic Books Subsidiary Rights: bookrights@natgeo.com

Designed by Chad Tomlinson

The publisher would like to thank Julie Beer, Michelle Harris, and Avery Hurt, authors and researchers; Grace Hill Smith, project manager; Emily Fego, project editor; Alison O'Brien Muff, photo editor; Lori Epstein, photo director; Amanda Larsen, art director; Julide Dengel, senior designer; Jennifer Geddes, fact-checker; Vivian Suchman, managing editor; Molly Reid, production editor; and Anne LeongSon and Gus Tello, associate designers.

Hardcover ISBN: 978-1-4263-7225-4
Reinforced library binding ISBN: 978-1-4263-7226-1

Printed in Hong Kong
22/PPHK/1